COMING OF AGE

My Journey to the Eighties

COMING OF AGE

My Journey to the Eighties

A MEMOIR

MADELEINE MAY KUNIN

GREEN WRITERS PRESS *Brattleboro, Vermont*

10 9 8 7 6 5 4 3 2 1

Green Writers Press is a Vermont-based publisher whose mission is
to spread a message of hope and renewal through the words and
images we publish. Throughout we will adhere to our commit-
ment to preserving and protecting the natural resources of the
earth. To that end, a percentage of our proceeds will be donated to
Emerge Vermont and the Institute for Sustainable Communities.
Green Writers Press gratefully acknowledges support from Cabot
Creamery Coop, individual donors, friends, and readers to help
support the environment and our publishing initiative.

GReen
wriTers
press

Giving Voice to Writers & Artists Who Will Make the World a Better Place
Green Writers Press | Brattleboro, Vermont
www.greenwriterspress.com

ISBN: 978-0-9994995-9-7

COVER: PHOTO BY TODD LOCKWOOD

PRINTED ON PAPER WITH PULP THAT COMES FROM FSC-CERTIFIED FORESTS, MANAGED FORESTS THAT
GUARANTEE RESPONSIBLE ENVIRONMENTAL, SOCIAL, AND ECONOMIC PRACTICES BY MCNAUGHTON & GUNN,
A WOMAN-OWNED BUSINESS CERTIFIED BY THE WOMEN'S BUSINESS ENTERPRISE NATIONAL COUNCIL.

To John W. Hennessey Jr.
1925-2018

ACKNOWLEDGMENTS

MY HUSBAND, JOHN, was my first reader—and he is the hero of this book. I thank Martha Kaplan, my agent, who believed in me, and Dede Cummings, my publisher, whose enthusiasm was inspirational. I am grateful to my editor, Rose Alexandre-Leach, and to Lali Cobb, who was my first editor. I thank the University of Vermont for naming me a Marsh Professor-at-large and giving me a place to work. I thank UVM staff members, including Kelly O'Malley, who came to my rescue when I had computer problems. I appreciate the Wake Robin community, who applauded my poetry readings. I thank several good friends who read parts of the manuscript and gave me valuable feedback. I am grateful to Liz Bankowski, who convinced me that there is an audience for a book on aging from a woman's perspective.

In a dream you are never eighty.

—ANNE SEXTON

CONTENTS

č

COMING OF AGE

My Journey to the Eighties

❦ Eighty-Four Years

Eighty-four years.
My birthday, big
as a stop sign
red, blazing.
The number blinks
and calls me
forward: *this is
who you are.*
I stop at the curb,
waiting for the
light to change,
to let me move on
like I always did
when I was forty-four
and green.

FOREWORD

ઽ

A S I ADJUST TO OLD AGE, I feel like Janus, looking in two directions at once, surveying my lengthy past and examining my foreshortened future. Death's black raven perches on my shoulder from time to time. Even when he flies away, I know he is in the neighborhood.

I wrote this memoir for the same reasons that all memoirs are written: to fulfill a need for self-definition, and because I wish to make sense of what is happening to me. I find that as I grow older I am more apt to take time to think about life and death. I have more time to turn inward. I am more avid for beauty. I spend time admiring trees (I have a favorite white boned sycamore). I watch the blue sky bloom sunset pink. I am not afraid of silence or stillness.

The coming-of-age memoir documents the rapid change from adolescence to adulthood; this coming-into-old-age memoir describes a slower and more subtle process. For my entire life, eighty has stood in the far distance, literally at the end of the road. I could barely see it or even think about it. Now it is here—a huge, looming number. My memoir takes the scattered events and thoughts of my life and sorts them within the covers of a book. It creates the happy illusion that life is an organized whole.

At this stage of my life I have accumulated enough titles to prompt the question, "What should I call you?" Titles do not grant immortality, but they provide a firm prop to keep my back straight. I have accumulated a few: wife, mother, state legislator, lieutenant governor, governor, US deputy secretary of education, ambassador to Switzerland, professor, poet, and writer. Two titles stick to me for life: governor and ambassador. They are preceded, however, by the word "former," which draws some of the air out. No matter what form of address precedes my name, I am, in my mid-eighties, indisputably, an old woman.

IN MIDLIFE, my day was propelled largely by outside forces. My schedule when I was governor was often divided into fifteen- and thirty-minute segments. I had to respond quickly to calls from reporters and demands from constituents—while juggling my family and career. My life was fragmented. Now, in my old age (these are still difficult words to put on paper), I am not in stasis, but I do have more time and desire to analyze and to write. Knowing that I have embarked on the last years of my life adds intensity to my days. The search for meaning that has often accompanied me in the past is now my frequent companion because the "end" is closer. Will I be around in five years, or ten years from now? I answer myself, *I do not know.*

What I do know is that I do not wish to live a long life, per se. I want to live a reasonably good life that allows me to cope with some expected losses of my senses but does not leave me totally blind, deaf, or immobile. My greatest fear is the loss of independence and the deterioration of my most vital organ: my mind.

It is impossible to imagine my future without me in it. So, I live in two different dimensions. One is like it always was: I greet the day with healthy anticipation; I do not dwell on limitations. The other radiates a sense of foreboding. When will I be unable to take care of myself? When will I die? How will I die? These questions do not frequently announce themselves, but they hover in the air.

When I was in my seventies, I attended a man's eightieth birthday party. I went because his wife was my friend and I thought he would not live much longer, and in fact he died within a year. That would never be me. Even when I looked at myself closely in the mirror and searched for evidence of age damage on my skin, it was as if I were scanning a white tablecloth for gravy spots. I could not see myself as the age I had become. How old was I? Fifty, or sixty, or perhaps seventy at most? Now, my wrinkles appear or disappear depending on the light. The photo on the cover of this book shows all my wrinkles. I seem proud of them, though I confess I don't always look or feel that way. I am not that accepting.

It is said that your life comes into focus on your deathbed, as it did for Tolstoy's Ivan Ilyich. I suggest that such questions begin to arrive much earlier. Now that I have passed eighty, I feel an urgency to describe my aging self before I reach my deathbed. I am focused on how it feels to be old. My knees creak when I get up from a deep chair, I feel my breath accelerate when I walk up a hill, and I feel a tremor in my hands when I sign my name.

Old age is often portrayed as a disease that can be prevented, or even cured, in a number of ways: anti-aging skin creams, vigorous exercise, plastic surgery, or even a pill. Youth and beauty are one in our society, and old age is the opposite. The adjectives "crone" and "hag" come to mind. Whistler's mother and Rembrandt's mother resemble one another: silent women, dressed in black. The desire to glorify youth and conquer aging is not new. Witness the sixteenth-century Spanish explorer Juan Ponce de León and his quest for the Fountain of Youth. The tourists who line up to see the site in St. Augustine, Florida, remind us that, five centuries later, we're still searching for the same. But the images in the media do not tell the real story of what it is to be old today. Old people are either portrayed as so fit and happy that they belong in Viagra advertisements, or they are shown suffering from excruciating pain in advertisements for arthritis medication.

This book does neither. I acknowledge the transformation that I am experiencing—physical, mental, and emotional. I regret my losses, but I do not linger there because the present pulls me in. I want to live in the here and now. I am greedy. The more life, the better. Still, I do not glorify old age. I see aging as a new stage of development during which I experience loss, but also continue to grow, learn, change, and find joy, even love. I am fortunate to have children, grandchildren, and a husband to hug; their love warms my life.

❦

WHEN I WAS YOUNG, the future was large. l wanted to grow into the next year quickly, to become an adult. Weeks were short because I had so much to do and not enough time. The future seemed infinite. Now I want time to slow down to a crawl, because I want more. In old age, my future has shrunk like a sweater steeped in hot water. It feels tight.

My priorities remain similar to what they were at a younger age, but now they take a different form. Instead of running for office myself, I pass the torch to a new generation of women. Five years ago, I founded Emerge Vermont, which recruits and trains women who want to run for public office. I want to help women discover their confidence and hone their skills. I have been urging women to enter public life ever since I was elected to the Vermont legislature in 1972; I think that being a mentor and role model may be my most important accomplishment. Women continue to feel they need accreditation before they dive into public life. Or they assume that a woman like me must be rich or have family connections. That has not been my story. My mother became a widow at an early age and my family had no political connections. Possibly it was idealism mixed with grit that pushed me to the podium.

I also find that I can write differently now than when I was involved in politics. Now my skin has become more translucent. I can be more personal. I don't wear the same shrink wrap I once sealed myself in. I can be more reckless about being judged. I no longer have to filter my words through a fine-meshed screen, leaving out phrases that might not please, or worse, offend and get me into trouble. My existence, when I was in public life, depended on public approval. I belonged to my audience. Out of public office, I belong more to myself. I can fling my arms wide when I want to, or I can keep them positioned at my side.

When old, old age arrives, I will want to be an overachiever. I want to score high on vitality, on curiosity. I remain curious about the new person, the new idea, the new day. I want to be around to see what happens next. When a resident at Wake Robin retirement community stops for a full fifteen seconds to hold the door for me, I thank him effusively. "Never mind," he replies. "I'm retired. I have nowhere else to go."

I think, *But I do, I do.*

❦ No Longer

No longer will we make love
before breakfast.
No longer will I dream
of seeing New Zealand
or the Cape of Good Hope.
Or bears in the wild.
No longer will I say
"Yes" more than "No."
No longer will danger sparkle
and safety look dull.
No longer will I look
at my body
without comparison
between who I was,
and who I have become,
blaming the light for
the difference.
No longer can I toss my hair
over my face,
and count one hundred strokes.

No longer can I do without
Night Cream and Day Cream,
slathering on, ounce after ounce.
No longer can I be comfortable
sitting in my chair, reading for hours
without getting up
to stretch my arms and legs.
No longer can I walk without
looking down at my feet
to avoid mean cracks and
malicious bumps.
No longer can I skip down
stairs like a girl, flying,
without feeling a thing.
No longer can I approach
the precipice without
swaying against my will.
No longer do I think ahead
of where I will be in ten years,
or twenty or more;

now I think in ones or twos or threes,
long enough to still hunger
for the food of life.
No longer do I wish for
the next day, or the next year,
to come quickly,
like I did the year
I turned ten.
I want the days to saunter,
like a leisurely
museum stroller who stops
now and then to gaze;
and get closer to the canvas
to see the brush strokes,
and then steps back
for the long view,
before moving on.

1

The Year I Turned Eighty

ಠ

T HE YEAR I TURNED EIGHTY, the color red
invaded my palette. I bought a new red Prius,
thinking it might be my last car. "Last car"
sounds like "last breath," and I wanted to go out in
a blast. If I hadn't worried about the wind further
destroying my hair, my ears, and my eyes, I would have
gone for a convertible.

I had owned my old Prius for nine years. It was
beige, and it blended silently in with the other cars in
the parking lot. Sometimes it took me several panicked
minutes (it has to be here somewhere) to find it in the

rows of vehicles. As I pushed my cumbersome shopping cart, I hoped no one would notice that I was lost, or rather, that my car was lost. My red car would be different—on the alert, happily signaling to me, even from a distance.

My new Prius was the color of the year: Barcelona Red. The marketing people had gotten it right. Not only did the name feel beautiful on the tongue, but Barcelona Red also evoked sunlit images of the time my second husband, John, and I visited Spain. The deep, vibrant red sparkled on the car lot. It was a young color. It had a touch of daring to it. I once had read that red cars are picked up more often for speeding than other colors. I was ready to take the risk. I wanted to defy the dark expectations of my age. Once I took it on the road, the rear view mirror showed me the standard gray interior, but when I looked at the side mirrors, I saw exactly what I wanted to see: a color that vibrates with life.

Red tempted me again as I decided on the colors of the walls and furniture fabrics of Wake Robin, a continuing care retirement community near Burlington, Vermont. The perfect cottage had become available, and my husband said that the time had come to make the move. I was less ready than he was to move to our final living space, but the fun of redecorating the cottage's four rooms eased the transition.

I had always thought white walls were perfect. That had been the color of the walls wherever I had lived—neutral, calm, and easy to live with. But now I wanted something bright, something that would bring the sun in and keep the gloom away. Yellow—that would be the color of every room except the kitchen, for which I chose a Tuscan red that was both calm and lively. That is what I had wanted: a kitchen different from the other kitchens at Wake Robin. But soon after it was painted, I saw the same color in several restaurants in Burlington and on the baseboards of the skilled nursing wing at Wake Robin. How original had I been?

The move to Wake Robin was a promising time in our lives. My husband had recently come out of a prolonged depression and had recovered from a bout of insomnia. We both agreed that the decision to move to Wake Robin had sparked his recovery. We had a plan for our old age. Our children would not be burdened when we reached that dreaded stage of dependence. If one of us died first, the other would not have to cope alone. The cottage was the most attractive one on campus. Tall trees framed it on two sides, and I could see the sunset through their silhouettes. There were lots of birds. But when I told a friend that we were moving to Wake Robin, she scoffed, "Oh, the old folks' home." I didn't think she was funny.

In preparation for the move, with my son Daniel's help, I bought some secondhand Danish modern in Montreal. I surprised myself by choosing the same style of furniture I had when I was married to Arthur, my former husband. When John and I married, we intermingled our possessions; he had a dark walnut table from his grandparents, and I had a spindly hand-painted Biedermeier writing desk and matching chairs from my Aunt Berthe. Our big joint investment would be two comfortable chairs. Money appeared to be no object, thanks to the stock market's recent surge and John's ebullient mood. He spotted the big, comfortable leather chair first, sat in it, and declared we should buy two for the study. I didn't think the study was large enough for two chairs with matching ottomans and suggested the living room instead. We didn't argue.

Together we looked over swatches of material. I didn't want leather, perhaps leather was a lifetime purchase and we did not have a lifetime. We did not inquire about warranties. We looked through books of swatches—lots of colors and a choice of fabrics. I spotted a bright red square and stopped. It leapt up at me.

I asked John, could we be bold and choose red? "Why not," he replied with his agreeable smile. I tried to picture the red chairs in our new living room. No question that they would be bright. No question that they would stand out. They would be contemporary. We would not be living in the past, surrounded only by possessions each of us had accumulated over fifty years. Our retirement home would be a sharp departure from that of the couple who had occupied it before us and had just been moved to assisted living. We were the young couple, moving in. I pushed away the questions: When would it be our turn? When would we have to move out to assisted living or skilled nursing in the Linden building? It had been hard for the other couple to leave. But they left nothing behind, and I was glad.

"Let's go for the red chairs," John and I agreed. The saleswoman was surprised, and I was pleased to see her reaction. We were not the beige, brown, or black-chair couple she had expected.

As the months went by waiting for the chairs to arrive, which had been specially ordered from Sweden, I began to have second thoughts. Would they work as I had anticipated, or would they be a disaster? Had we decided too quickly? Why hadn't I deliberated longer, given darker colors a chance? When the chairs arrived, shrink-wrapped in heavy plastic, the two men who unloaded them had to use a knife to release them from bondage. There they stood: two solid walls of red.

"They're so big," I exclaimed. "They looked different in the showroom."

My husband was dismayed. He had had a relapse of his insomnia and depression. "They're not what I expected either," he said. The chairs blazed in the room. I had hoped they would cure his insomnia and cheer him up, but instead they wore him down. They wore me down.

We tried placing one chair in the living room and the other in the study. Better, but not right. My stepdaughter came to fix the computer and sat in one of the chairs. "I like them. They're comfortable."

"Really?" I questioned.

John and I became obsessed with the red chairs. We talked about them over breakfast, lunch, and dinner. I would take a look at them before going to bed and again first thing in the morning, in case they looked any better. They didn't. "Let's stop talking about the chairs," John said as his insomnia weakened him.

"Yes, we won't talk about them anymore," I agreed, but it was hard.

I called the furniture store to ask if we could return

them. The owner was properly dismayed. He was polite, and didn't want to displease a customer, but clearly he was upset. "Keep them until Monday and then tell me what you think," he suggested.

The next day I placed a square black pillow with a brilliant red flower leaping to the edges in the corner of our beige couch. My son Daniel had given it to us as a housewarming gift. It lifted the couch out of its neutrality and tied it to the red chairs—a sudden improvement.

My son Adam came to dinner and my friend Veronica stopped by. Adam sat in one chair and Veronica in the other. The chairs looked different when someone sat in them. Their bodies blotted out much of the red. The color formed a frame.

"I like them," Veronica exclaimed, resting her elbows comfortably on the armrests as she leaned back. She was used to bulky furniture. Her taste is not my taste, I silently demurred. "Two thumbs up!" my son said. "If you don't like the color, you can get slipcovers." His wife had done that with their cat-scratched couch. True, but why slipcover new chairs?

I looked at the chairs once more. I asked myself whether I could ever own them. Would I feel comfortable, or would they always jolt me, make me jumpy, on edge? Why hadn't I chosen the light, neutral textures with which I had surrounded myself in the past—silent, relaxing colors that made the living room a calm refuge from the harsh and noisy world outside?

Part of me, I realized, no longer wanted a refuge. I wanted to bring life inside, not leave it at the door. And the red chairs did exactly that. They were loud. They were vivid. Day by day, I began to see that they had precisely what I wanted: brilliance. One bright morning, my husband and I arrived at the same decision.

"Let's keep them."

ℰ THE BED

These were my sheets and his bed.
These are not the right sheets, he said,
letting the corner limp down over the edge.
Just tuck them in, I said, with a hint of annoyance
that he didn't know better. They always fit on my bed.
I said exactly what I thought, knowing that I might
not be understood, or worse, offend.
There was a slight grating echo in our words
which we heard in different ways.
In other times, with other people, it would have
shredded the tie that bound them, but in this
time, with the two of us, the tear was so
quickly rewoven, that we looked at each other
and laughed.

2

I Am Not Old

𝓔

I COULD BE THE OLDEST PERSON IN THE AUDIENCE, but so what. My age drops to the floor and I step on it with my dancing feet. Mavis Staples is shaped like a muffin, dressed in a swishy black top and matching and swinging black silk pants. Her hair is like a blonde bowl. It sparkles. She is escorted onstage by the hand of a dark-suited assistant. She needs help, but when the band starts to jive, she rolls across the stage like a loose marble.

Her shoulders pump up and down to the music, her arms are swinging, and her feet kick off gravity. Then she opens her mouth and out it comes: a powerful voice that blasts into the crowd. She's got it, they clap, she's still got it!

"How old is she?" I ask the woman sitting next to me, who seems to know all the songs.

"I don't know," she replies.

I guess. Mavis tells the audience that the Staple Singers have been singing for sixty-five years. Let's see, eighty, or eighty-five, maybe?

"I'm so excited," Mavis exclaims more than once between songs.

She is outrageously happy. Then she pauses, spotting a familiar face in the audience, and reaches down. He jumps on the stage. Tall, dressed in white pants and jacket, with lanky long hair, he runs to her side and hugs her. They sing a song or two together, and then they dance.

"Did you see me dance?" she coquettishly asks the audience. "I almost fell down, but he held me up."

I clap with the crowd, moving my feet and shoulders, trying to keep up.

The crowd hoots and hollers. I release my voice. I shout, surprising myself.

When the bass guitarist has a solo, he bends his body in like a straw. He holds his instrument in a lover's embrace. He makes it sing in a high-pitched voice, a voice so beautiful, so plaintive, like the singing of a loon.

The drummer has his turn. He builds up the sound to a mad tempo, like jazz drummers do, but this time, perhaps because his hair is white, I pound the drums with him. I allow myself to drum the hell out of those drums. It feels so good.

I am not old.

ꙮ When I Was Sick

When I was sick with stinging cramps
  I could not carry my eyelids open.
My intestines were like helpless
  pebbles tossed in swirls.
I promised myself
  that when I returned to
    the land of the well,
I would secrete gratitude
  from every pore—
God, she, he, whoever.
I would take a deep breath,
  deeper than everyday breath,
and exhale a bellows-full that
  could blow your house down.
I would thank God, or someone
  very much like her,
    for being alive, a while longer.
I would look at the lake until I was bored;
  I would rest my eyes
    where the sea and the sky meet.
I would be content,
  with breathing in and breathing out.

3

Attraction

❡

A FTER MY HUSBAND'S SURGERY, the neu-
rosurgeon walks into the examining room
wearing the power of his knife. He does not
need to swagger. He wears his magic comfortably, and I
give him everything he could have asked for—respect,
deference, even adoration—because his hands have
saved John's life. That does not stop me from admiring his handsome tie, his well-tailored navy suit, and
his almost portly body. I wonder if he flirts with the
nurses, if he has a wife and if she is attractive, if she is a
stay-at-home wife or has her own career.

"You're looking good," he says to John as he sits down on a stool across from him, legs splayed.

Then he turns to me. "You always look good."

I smile, pleased, attracted.

In the car on the way home, after John has been safely buckled in the front seat and the walker folded into the trunk, I wonder when the zing of attraction will become dull.

I have less need for anonymous touch than I did during the ten years that I was single. Yes, as my husband has aged into infirmity, I do miss sex, not just the physical sensation, but the closeness John and I felt when we became lovers. But I can look back now to how I felt when John and I made love, folded together, skin against skin, sealed in love.

We didn't fuck; we made love. I still rarely use the "F" word. It doesn't come naturally to me. "Fuck" retains its shock value, even when it is blurted out without any reference to sex. Only when I watch a movie where "fuck" is used as often as "and" and "the," does it become devoid of its meaning and into an act of aggression.

When I was becoming sexually aware, women were not supposed to be sexual creatures. Lust was reserved for men. Oddly enough, it is as we get older that we can say to ourselves, *yes, we are.* Jane E. Brody, health columnist for the *New York Times*, wrote what I already know: older people still enjoy making love, but we're not supposed to talk about it.

The sensation of touch is a fundamental human need. Some women go to the hairdresser or get a manicure or a massage to find touch from a stranger. A doctor's stethoscope can occasionally satisfy the hunger. One night during cocktails before dinner, after having spoken at a symposium, I found myself talking to a tall, middle-aged German scientist who had made a fascinating presentation on cook stoves and indoor pollution. I felt a special rapport with him. We stood in a corner, apart from the others. I took another sip of champagne and smiled when he complimented me on my outfit: a green silk jacket and my favorite suede boots—tall, forest green, trimmed with black leather, like a riding boot.

"You are the most fashionably dressed woman here. And you keep yourself looking so well."

I felt a flutter of flirtation go through me and waited expectantly for what he might say next.

"So many German women let themselves go when they get older. They wear shapeless black dresses. Unlike you." He paused and looked into my eyes. "You remind me of my mother."

"Oh."

❦

WHEN I PUSH JOHN'S WHEELCHAIR, the top of his bald head looks up at me—a pale, clear landing field where I plant a kiss. I cannot see his face, but I hear his response: "Thank you." My lips part. Even in my eighties I am capable of attraction, susceptible to flattery, something stirs.

Now I seek out his hands when they are within reach. At a performance of *La traviata*, I reach across my seat to his lap, and his hands sandwich mine. Dying Violetta's aria floods both our bodies. I feel his strength—one hand pressing down from above, the other providing warmth from below. We are clasped. It isn't sex, it isn't making love, but it is good.

ℰ Can There Be More to Say

Can there be more to say after
we have said everything there
is to say about oatmeal, warm toast,
and sliced bananas?
The weather has words.
I find them and report
that I wear gloves
but no boots, not yet.
He is inside and I am out
where the air is colder
than it was yesterday.
Chances of snow
mixed with rain.
One never knows
which way it will come down.
We have no plans that
have to be changed.
We talk about dinner:
what time, what place,
dining room or café?
Small morsels of words fill
us up until we pause,
take a breath, and devour
another sentence.

4

The Cane, the Walker, the Wheelchair

ቈ

I REACH OUT to hold my husband's hand during a concert, a private gesture in a public space. Sometimes I just lean into him, enjoying the feeling of our shoulders touching. I push gently in and he pushes lightly back. We listen to the music through each other's bodies, an ethereal way to make love.

We talk about who will die first. It is a difficult conversation because, even at our ages, being in love has made us push death into the background. We pretend that we will live forever. The final stretch of life that lies before us is a gift that we know will expire. John suggests that I engrave the words "carpe diem" on my wedding band. I inscribe the same words on a paper-weight I give him for his birthday.

Sometimes I wish to die first so I will not have to lose him, but it is more likely that he will die first because he is almost nine years older than me. Whatever happens, I will have had the unexpected experience of our love-filled marriage. I will have known what love is at the closing chapters of my life. I will always remember John's presence, as I still feel my brother's. I don't want to probe the inevitability of death further. Not now. We both overslept this morning.

JOHN'S HEALTH began to decline soon after we returned from a ten-day vigil at my dying brother's bedside in Tucson, Arizona. When we got home, John was diagnosed with pneumonia. His body was severely weakened and he had difficulty sleeping. He could not travel to Edgar's memorial service with me because I had to leave early and return late from Springfield, which was less than two hours away. I was grateful to good friends who drove him there just in time for the service and brought him back right after, holding onto his arm to keep his body steady. We had planned that he would come to Oxford University with me for a symposium on women and children's health in which I would participate. He had to cancel. It took him several months to recover. Now that I look back, I see that he never completely recovered.

It was the beginning of a life that moved in cycles, good months alternating with bad months. Over time it turned into good weeks, then days, and then hours. He became unsteady on his feet. He had trouble getting a good night's sleep. The most mysterious and intractable symptom was a black depression that periodically overwhelmed him. When the depression lifted, he was exuberant. We could do anything. Upon my return from Oxford, he proposed that we make the move to Wake Robin. He had found the perfect cottage, the best one by far. If moving to Wake Robin would make him happy, I readily agreed. Then, a month later, just before our new chairs arrived, he became anxious. Was this the right move? How could we furnish our new place; what would we take from our condo? As his anxiety increased day by day, I took more responsibility for the move, trying to assure him that everything would go smoothly, even though I myself had doubts.

By the beginning of March his mood had lifted, and he proposed that we travel around the world on the Queen Mary II. I looked at the itinerary and started to imagine us in all the places I had always wanted to see: Hong Kong, New Zealand, Australia, and the Cape of Good Hope. How exciting! Three weeks ago he hadn't wanted to go to the store to buy milk and orange juice. Now he buys three of each. I tell him that we can't fit them in the refrigerator, but he just smiles and I smile back. So what if the refrigerator is too full and the milk turns sour? He is out of his depression. We share kisses, morning, noon, and night, punctuating them with the words, I love you, to assure one another, to reassure ourselves. We are near delirious with refound happiness. The sky is bluer, and the grass, greener.

Then he began to approach ninety. He said, "I ignore birthdays. I don't want a party, please don't do anything," so we had a nice dinner, just the two of us. I had written a poem to mark the day, and he accepted it as "the best present," holding his magnifying glass steady over each word while I waited for his smile.

But he could not put a stop to birthdays. Neither could he climb fully out of his depression. He could no longer make decisions about our move to Wake Robin: what colors to paint the walls, how to pick out carpeting, and how to connect our phones. We couldn't get cell phone connection. Our computers didn't work. Every glitch became a monster. My stepdaughter spent days trying to get everything to work.

Totally frustrated, John could not sleep past one or two in the morning. He lifted himself from the bed slowly, as if there were too many thick blankets bearing down on him. The weight burdened him all day. His spirit became mummified in layers of cotton. He was inside his depression, and I was left outside. I could not reach in to pull him out.

Instead of rescuing him, I found myself slipping in. Depression can morph into a communicable disease. "How was your night?" I asked each morning, making my voice cheerful with expectation. I already knew it was bad when I saw how his body was positioned next to me: face down, one hand holding his forehead as if trying to wipe away his nighttime torment. Evenings were always better. As the night sky darkened, his mood would begin to lighten. We could converse. Sometimes he would lie about how he felt and I knew it was for my sake. He wanted to spare me. I didn't contradict him. When he said he felt better, my guilt was eased. My love should cure him; I should be able to seduce him into a sweet sleep and a fresh awakening.

The mention of insomnia in conversations with other people brought out all sorts of advice. I listened eagerly. Soak your feet in hot water. Drink hot milk. Read a book. Play this CD. Count backwards by seven. Medications, old and new, were prescribed. And then there were things not to do: Don't watch the evening news. Don't read on your Kindle. Don't exercise at night. We consulted his family doctor, a geriatric therapist, and a psychiatrist. We spent much of August of 2014 traveling back and forth for treatments at Dartmouth Hitchcock Medical Center. Then, one morning after a two-hour session with a new doctor and an increase in medication, it happened again.

"How was your night?"

"Wonderful."

That morning he cleared his desk of all the accumulated correspondence and quickly went through his e-mail. He bought three pairs of bedroom slippers online and sent them back the following day, still looking for exactly what he wanted. He went with me to buy flowers; he made plans to have dinner with people every night; he wrote a poem for the first time and read it aloud to me; he fixed the CD player; he listened to Mahler the entire day. His study was now perfectly organized. Two weeks ago, nothing was in the right place.

"It's a miracle," I said to the doctor, wishing to bless him. He only nodded. He knew better. Still, he assured us that the depression was not likely to return. I wanted so badly to believe him.

A month later, the beast had him "by the neck" (John's words). He had bad nights. Nightmares woke him up, carving deep crevices on either side of his face. Desperate for relief, we both agreed to go forward with electroconvulsive therapy (ECT), despite my reservations. My father had been treated with electroconvulsive therapy when it was in its primitive stage, and I remembered that my mother had referred to it with horror. My son, a doctor, supported ECT for John, and so did my stepdaughter Martha. I relinquished my hesitation because I wanted John to walk out of the cave and emerge as my husband, the man I knew, the man I had married.

So much hope is placed in doctors' hands. We endow them with magical powers. I believed in magic after the first recovery. We both did. And then poof, the wand went dead. We endured eight sessions of ECT, driving for two hours back and forth to Hanover, New Hampshire, and staying overnight at Martha's house in time for treatments at six in the morning. After each treatment, I fed him bits of blueberry muffin like a child and he swallowed them with sips of water. Each time he awoke from the anesthesia, I expected to see the smile of salvation on his face. Cured! Not yet. Patience, patience.

John became more prone to losing his balance. A fall, I feared, could kill him. My arm was in a constant state of readiness. A low level of anxiety permeated our partnership. If he fell when I was with him, it would be my fault. If he fell when I was not with him, it would also be my fault, only more so. I found myself, as an old woman, reliving the tension I had experienced as a young woman. Should I give myself to the children, or should I venture out to my own life? We were fortunate to be at Wake Robin where help was always available. How terrible I had felt when I did not get home from giving a speech in time to watch my son blow out his nine birthday candles. I should have been there when I was elsewhere. Now the same dilemma haunted me. Should I go to my office and write, have lunch with friends, feed my own soul? Bad mother, neglectful wife, selfish woman.

John did not keep me bound to his side. "Go," he would say, "you've got to do your work." It was I who imprisoned myself. I would call him frequently when I was not with him. If there was no answer on his cell phone, I called the landline. Again, no answer. I told myself that he must be taking a nap. But what if he'd fallen? What if he couldn't reach the emergency button hanging from his neck? I called again, both numbers. And he answered. He was safe. I was safe.

John began using a cane. He often forgot to use it or misplaced it. When it fell down from where it had been propped—a table, a chair, a counter—I jumped at the sound of the crash. "Are you alright?" I developed a sixth sense, not for my body but for his. I felt like a mother watching her toddler take his first steps, ready to catch him at any moment, arms outstretched. The toddler wobbles, falls, and stands up again, laughing. Now John is in reverse, back to the wobbly stage, and no longer cushioned by laughter. When we walk arm in arm instead of using the cane, it could be mistaken for romance. Sometimes we hold hands, firmly. We have become an old couple, an obstacle in the way. I tell John a cane is elegant; it looks good on him. I have a photo of my father standing still for the photographer on a hiking path in the Alps, his cane planted at a rakish angle, as was the fashion.

Months later, Martha gives us the walker of a neighbor who has died. But I don't want it in the house. No, we don't need it, thank you. I put it in the garage. Then I begin to recognize the obvious: I can't anticipate a fall. By its very nature, a fall is sudden, shocking. Still, I can't help asking, too often, "Are you stable, are you alright?" The words became a wearisome mantra. I make the decision to get a walker. (The one in the garage had been given to a tag sale.) Whether he likes it or not, I will get him a walker. I have counted five falls in two weeks. He would list to the right and to the left like a sail, and then capsize. I have become expert at placing ice packs on his bruises and Band-Aids on his wounds. Nothing has broken, not yet.

Just before the start of the Labor Day weekend, I rush to the rehabilitation center at Wake Robin and request a walker. Reluctantly, John agrees to try it out. When he places his hands on the two handlebars, he smiles. I smile. He will be safe. I alone am no longer responsible for his safety. The walker is my friend. John agrees that graduating to a walker does not mark the end stage of his life. Walkers are parked everywhere at Wake Robin, lined up like alert soldiers. He treats his like a new toy, and I have to slow him down when we walk to our cottage. We joke about speed limits.

One day after dinner I suggest that we walk around the semicircle of our cottages. The doctor has recommended more exercise to improve his stability. With the walker, we will be fine. I stop to look at a neighbor's window to assess the progress of their renovations. "Not much going on," I say.

John takes one hand off the walker to take a look. He begins to sway, gently at first, as if he might right himself. I stretch my arms out to him, but I can't reach him in time. He falls, slowly it seems, but he hits the sidewalk hard.

"Are you hurt?" I ask several times, hoping for the right answer.

"Yes."

"Where does it hurt, John?" He can't say. I manage to pull him to his feet and we walk with my arm around his waist and his arm around mine. We head for our door. Panic practically fells me. What if this fall had been "it"? What if I had killed him? In my mind I replay the video of his fall again and again. I had been transfixed in disbelief as I watched him go down. I thought he would stop. But he didn't.

"It was my fault," I lament.

When we arrive at our cottage, step by careful step, he says, "I've got to lie down." He didn't say that after previous falls. He is pale and shaken. He has hit the right side of his head—not too hard, I think—but a bump is beginning to swell. I get the icepack and put it on his forehead. He complains of chest pain, possibly a broken rib. Should I press the emergency button, the button I had once dismissed as unnecessary? We didn't need it then, but we do now. I find the emergency pendant hanging in the bathroom and press the blue center twice. It seems longer, but it takes only a few minutes for a man from Emergency Services to knock

43

on our door. We speak briefly and conclude that John should go to the emergency room. I see the flashing red ambulance from the window. Two uniformed EMTs, a man and a woman, pull the oversized stretcher into the bedroom. So that's what the wide doors are for.

I am instructed to follow in my car, but not to go through any red lights. I promptly disobey and keep up with the ambulance, wondering if the flashing lights are routine or an indication that John is badly hurt. But we are lucky. The x-rays show no broken bones. John can go home.

But this was John's sixth fall. My doctor son, Adam, and the attending physician recommend that John not return to our cottage but go to the skilled nursing unit at Wake Robin instead. There he will be protected from further falls and receive physical therapy. I agree, feeling both guilt and relief. Our relationship is changing; he will live in one place, and I—no matter how close by—will live in another. He is entering a state of dependency, a state he will grow to hate.

We have one more night in the same bed; the nurses can't admit him until the next morning. I sniff his clean body. I feel his hand rest on my thigh. I reach out for his shoulder and listen to his breath. When will we be blanketed together like this again? He gets up three times in the night, at three, four, and five o'clock, to go to the bathroom. I have asked him to wake me up each time so that he will not stumble in the night. In the morning we are both exhausted. Still, it doesn't seem reason enough to move him to skilled nursing. But we go, he with both hands on the walker, me with one hand on his arm.

I give him up.

But only for the time being. He moves back to the cottage. Then he falls again, and begins shuffling his feet when he walks. New x-rays yield a diagnosis of a subdural hematoma caused by falls. An operation follows, and a slow recovery. Our lives are cyclical: brief recoveries when we dream about sailing on the Queen Mary II, and then the nightmares repeat themselves.

One night when John is in skilled nursing, I improvise. I ask a nurse to place a white tablecloth on a round table in the activity room. I set a bottle of red wine in the center and take the blue and white china plates out from my tote bag and frame them with silver knives and forks and blue linen napkins. Then I walk down the hall to John's room, number 205.

"Dinner is ready," I announce like a butler. He rises from his chair carefully, every motion mentally rehearsed before translation into movement. He grasps both handles of the walker, steadies himself, and takes the first step to set the others in motion. He cannot,

45

will not, fall. I walk by his side, mimicking his rhythm. We reach the make-believe dining room and John expresses delighted surprise.

"How did you do this?"

"I got permission. I brought a picnic."

It's Sunday night, the only night when no dinner is served for residents. He could have had dinner with the other nursing home patients at four thirty in the afternoon, but we rebel against institutional time and besides, I wanted to cook. I had clipped a new recipe from the *New York Times*: velvet chicken, plus my favorite vegetable, parsnips, and his favorite, spinach. I didn't have all the ingredients for the chicken. I used flour instead of cornstarch, light cream instead of crème fraiche, and omitted thyme out of necessity. I was generous with the Dijon mustard.

When I open the plastic containers, a lovely aroma swims over the table. I spoon the food onto the plates, careful to make them equal. I wish I had brought candles. But they aren't needed. We create our own light. I drink two glasses of red wine alone. John has to abstain because the doctor said alcohol interferes with his medication. We make a toast, wine clicking with water.

"To your health," I say.

"To your health," he replies, and gives me one of his warm smiles. I kiss him in return.

ℰ CHRYSALIS

You came out of it
born anew, like
yesterday, almost
not quite, but
good enough for me.
How did you claw your
way out from the chrysalis?
Scratching all that time,
scratching . . . scratching
until you caught a thread
that unraveled into sight
and sound, until you slid
back to me, arms
outstretched,
wavering in the air,
until the ground rose
up to our feet.

5
Late in Life Love

ც

I WAS SEVENTY-ONE and had been on my own for ten years when I fell in love. Like most women that age, I had secretly hoped it would happen but never seriously expected it to. I had watched my older brother court a variety of girlfriends after his wife had moved to Washington and he was virtually single. He was a successful seducer; women fell for him regardless of their age or his.

He confided in me, "It's much harder for women," and I soberly agreed while feeling envious of his ability to behave like an old rooster. Some years after my divorce I had begun to peruse dating sites. I knew that they produced many wonderful romances, but I dared not enter my name for fear I would be discovered: "Former Vermont governor, late sixties, looking for . . ."

I first came across the name John Hennessey when a generous check came in the mail for my lieutenant governor's campaign in 1978. It was from New Hampshire. I learned that John and his wife, Jean, were strong supporters of Democrats, and female Democrats in particular. The checks kept coming when I ran for governor. What if I hadn't accepted John's invitation to join the advisory board of Americans for Campaign Reform, a new organization he and others were launching? What if I hadn't met him for lunch the following fall after his wife had died? What if I hadn't said yes when he wanted to brief me on the organization's recent developments? What if I hadn't had an extra ticket in my purse for the Vermont Symphony Orchestra's performance that night?

"What's the program?" John prudently asked.

"Beethoven's Ninth."

What if he hadn't loved Beethoven's Ninth?

People began to see us sitting together at the symphony. A year later, as we were walking in the rain to another performance, a young woman rushed by us and exclaimed, "I'm on my way to the symphony, to meet the man of my dreams."

John is the man of my dreams. It was serendipity that brought us together. Neither of us calls on God very often, but we both believe in destiny. It had to be. Although we had lived separate lives for so many years (seventy for me, almost eighty for him), we had been at some of the same places, had read the same books, enjoyed the same music, and had visited the same museums. Most importantly—and unexpectedly, since John was the former dean of Dartmouth's Tuck School of Business—we had the same liberal Democratic politics. And John liked strong women, something that his first wife, Jean, and I had in common. He, not I, would refer to God as "she." When we explored the past, we found so many common threads that it was as if we had led parallel lives. "I can give you ten years," he said, when we agreed to get married. That seemed like forever.

John, who would shortly turn eighty, was remarkably young for his age. Mentally alert, physically strong, we could do everything together. Unlike younger couples who struggle to achieve a balance between work and life, we were unencumbered by young children or career ambition. We traveled to all the places we wished to go: Switzerland, England, Egypt, China, Italy, France, India, and more. John accompanied me on all my book tours in every part of the country and kept four-by-six note cards about every event, jotting down the date, place, names, and reaction to my speeches. He kept his admiring eyes on me the whole time I spoke, never looked bored or fell asleep, and would give me instant feedback about my talk, almost always laced with praise. He edited my writing. He was, indeed, the perfect partner, intellectually, emotionally, and romantically. John would say to me, "I know you," and he did.

How often did we say how lucky we were to have found one another? We felt like young lovers. And we must have looked the part. Our heads bent close in conversation in a restaurant prompted a young couple to stop at our table.

"How long have you two been together?" I think they expected at least fifty years.

"Just six years. This is our second marriage."

They did not evidence disappointment. "I hope we'll be like you when we grow old."

❦ I Loved You When You Did the Dishes

I cooked, you did the dishes.
Did I love you for that?
I listened to the distant
clattering in the kitchen
while I sat in my chair,
reading the newspaper.
We shared most tasks then,
but you did the driving
and I could sit
still by your side,
with only a rare glance in
the rearview mirror to
check if it was safe to pass.
Now I do everything:
cook and wash the pots
and meet
the dishwasher's
greedy demands.
I make the bed, which you once
made when we slept together.

I push your wheelchair,
and straighten my back,
not letting it sink
into a stoop
before its time.
I feel my muscles tighten,
up the incline;
I wish you could feel it, too,
from your glued position.
You need me now to move
in any direction:
up and down,
and around corners,
without bumping into
things, like winter boots,
thrown casually on the floor.
I take the lead, pulling
you out of yourself, and into
the world I inhabit.
You visit me, from time to time,

like you used to do
when you did the dishes,
and the counters always
needed wiping.

This evening is better than
this morning, when you berated yourself
for growing old.
"What can I do?" you asked,
pleading with yourself.
I whispered, "Nothing."
Evenings we meet on the sofa
and talk about a story in the *New York Times*.
Or a scene from the evening news.
We are same-minded again;
the world is spinning
crazily, out of its orbit.
We shake our heads
from side to side
in rhythmic disbelief.
I reach for your still hand,
cover it with mine,
and keep it there.

6

Fat Backs

ح

I NOTICE OTHER WOMEN'S BACKS IN THE SWIMMING POOL, some mottled with bean-size freckles that merge into each other, others rising like soft dough. After my shower, holding my thick yellow towel, I turn in front of the mirror and look at my own. I discover a small ridge that sags out from under my bathing suit, just under my arms. I tuck it in on both sides. I face the mirror and detect a new hint of cracked glass patterned on my chest. I apply more body lotion. My skin could be the subject of endless examination. Silky, crepey skin suddenly appears on my upper arms when I hold them close to my body. Little red spots dot my torso, light brown patches mark my cheeks, and the lines on my face deepen like parched earth.

A half-moon starts from under my breasts, curves over my navel, and ends a few inches above my pubic bone. I suck it in whenever I think about it, which is not often enough. I can accept my changed body when I stand squarely in front of the mirror; I still have a waistline, after all. But in profile, I am oval. This does not completely surprise me except that my new profile is so solid.

Do I scrutinize my body more carefully now that I am growing out of it than when I was in adolescence and growing into it? I still like to look attractive, so I put myself together more carefully now than I did before. I am aware that morsels of food can slip off my fork and land in my lap. I check for stains surreptitiously, not wanting anyone to notice when I dip the corner of my linen napkin into my water glass to scrub away a spot. An older woman who is slovenly is either oblivious to how she looks, or she is no longer able to take care of herself. Not me. Never mind the wrinkles, the blue-veined hands, the sagging chin—I remain a proud, even a vain, woman.

℘

WHEN I WAS YOUNG and pregnant we wore smocks and enormous flowing dresses. I made some myself with yards and yards of material to hide my swollen body; the connection between intercourse and pregnancy was one we did not want to advertise. The words "baby bump" or "having sex" were not in our vocabulary. Today the sight of a decidedly pregnant woman in the locker room, wearing a red bikini that covers only five percent of her body, makes me look twice.

When we were young, those who developed breasts early, like my friend Nina, tried to hide them. Her mother made her special outfits, something like maternity dresses, to hide her embarrassing bumps. I was not eager to be like Nina and made to suffer from the crude remarks hurled by our classmate Burton Strumpf. "Can I milk you?" Ugh.

I was most conscious of my height in elementary school. Whenever we marched out of our classroom we were lined up according to size. I was grateful to Myra Wigdor for saving me from being last. She had the further distinction of having one blue eye and one brown eye. My height became even more burdensome in high school and college. "How tall is he?" was the first question I would ask before agreeing to go out on a blind date. I fully accepted the stereotypical model of the perfect couple: taller man, shorter woman. That image is imprinted everywhere, even the yellow and black street-crossing signs. The photograph I wanted to create was that of a wedding cake pair.

My first husband was my height when we got married. But then he shrank, and I worried that next to him I might look bossy or domineering, a battle axe. I liked the idea of having a tall, strong protector (a father, at last), but I didn't want to be bound by him. I wanted to keep my independence within the folds of security. There is safety in stereotypes.

When I was campaigning for governor, I worked diligently to craft an economic development speech that I was going to present to a largely male, blue-suited audience. I anxiously wondered how they would react. I was thrilled when I heard the applause at the end. Still basking in my victory, I saw an acquaintance coming towards me with a big smile on his face. Great, I thought, he liked it. He shook my hand.

"Madeleine, I just love your hair."

I have heard that audiences are more affected by how a speaker looks than by what is being said. When

I entered politics, my staff received a call in the middle of a gubernatorial campaign—"Tell her not to wear gray stockings"—and I knew I had to stick to my uniform: neutral stockings, small-heeled shoes, a dark suit, a sensible blouse with no cleavage, and for variety, I could add a bright scarf. The message was, *Don't stand out.* I was on a teeter-totter: not too feminine and not too masculine, just enough of each gender to look like a real governor (male) and still be true to myself (female). The test is authenticity. The parameters of success are narrow. Too masculine, and I would be aloof, or cold. Too feminine, and I would be too soft and weak. We must appear tough yet soft, distant yet approachable, beautiful, but not too beautiful. Women leaders have to carefully calibrate what they wear, as Hillary Clinton, trapped in a black pantsuit most days, knows. Because the public is not familiar with a woman assuming a traditionally male role, a silent question is often asked: Is she real, or is she faking it?

Age, and no longer running for office, has liberated me from some of these burdens. Now that I am in my eighties, I am delighted to be tall. In my aerobics class I welcome compliments about my posture, and I admit to purposely straightening up and stretching my stride when I pass a row of men and women pushing their walkers. And I can wear patterned stockings, short or long skirts, red shoes, and change my hairstyle whenever I wish. When I recently spoke to a group of former women governors, a question came from the audience about proper clothes. I shared my experience and then blurted out, "Now that I'm no longer in office, I don't have to give a damn."

ℰ Hands

The woman sitting next to me
has purple-veined hands,
thick as ropes.
I look at my hands,
only a shade lighter.
Inky veins bulging
out of my paper skin.
How could I be
almost like her?

7

The Manicure,
My Mother

ु

W HEN I AM GETTING A MANICURE, I am my mother. Her hands are now my hands. My veins rise up from my wax-paper skin, like hers did. My fingers are long. I like to wear tight black gloves that silhouette their shape. I once thought my hands destined me for the piano. I was to be disappointed. Still, I am vain about them. It's possible that my father had beautiful hands too, but there is no way to know. His portrait shows his hands folded in his lap, curved over a newspaper. They could be any shape. I must have felt them when he held me in his arms and when I learned to walk, holding on tight to him with one hand and my mother with the other. I have a photo of my brother like that.

I was both my mother's daughter and her close companion. Because my brother was four years older, I was loved almost like an only child. My mother did not always want to venture out by herself, and so we did things together like two girlfriends. We rode the first car of the subway together into Manhattan, standing in front of the window to watch the tunnel opening up and the bright lights switching on and off. We went to Broadway theatres together when a ticket for $2.80 bought a better seat than one that cost $1.20. We saw *La bohème* together, and I was embarrassed when the curtain went up after the final act and I couldn't hide the tears running down my face. Poor Mimi.

A special treat was to go to Radio City Hall to see a movie and a show. We would stand in line for hours. That is where I saw my first movie; Carmen Miranda was the star and I was mesmerized by the basket of fruit she balanced on her head while she twisted and turned to a rumba. After the show we went to Schrafft's, where the sun shone in through large picture windows. I ordered a coffee ice-cream soda and we watched the clusters of crowds walk down Broadway from our window table.

When I was almost fifteen, I had a crush on a seventeen-year-old boy who I believed was a genius. We met in the Catskills when my mother and his parents became friends. He played Rachmaninoff with great speed while he leant in towards the music. He painted with oils. He was slim and dark haired, and his name was Francis Mechner. My mother bought one of his dark, green landscapes for fifteen dollars. One night he offered to walk me home from his house to ours. I was thrilled. My mother quickly said no need, that the two of us would go home together. I found it hard to forgive her.

When I was fifteen, my mother bought a white house with green shutters and a screened-in porch on Foote Avenue in Pittsfield, Massachusetts. "Life will be easier," is how she described the move. We would be close to family. And so we left our sixth-floor apartment in New York for the small town where my mother's nephew Ernest, his wife, Ruth, and their two children had recently settled.

In moving, my mother was leaving behind a clutch of Swiss women who lived in an apartment building like ours, but down the street. They were better off than we were. My mother couldn't keep up with them. She was always worried about our finances and sought advice from any relative or close friend. The women spoke the Swiss dialect amongst themselves, but my mother was anxious to perfect her English. She was determined to lose her accent. I was embarrassed by it. Only much later did I hear my friends say that my mother's accent was charming. By then, it was.

I think my mother experienced more than anxiety. My father's suicide had left its scar: life could end in an instant. Perhaps she thought that if she had exercised more caution, she could have saved him. She was *ängstlich*, which is the German word for anxiety plus fear. I tried to inoculate myself against it because I sensed that it could foreshorten my future. I was daring on roller skates, and good at jump rope, but on the P.S. 101 playground I could not conquer the metal jungle gym bars. Other girls could hang by their knees and swing back and forth, letting their dresses hang down, but I was terrified to let go.

I often wondered, and later began to understand, the strength required of my mother to take me, at six and a half years old, and my brother, aged ten, to America to escape the threat of Hitler's invasion. We waved goodbye to our friends and relatives at the Zürich train station and boarded the S.S. Manhattan in Genoa. My mother had thought we had a private cabin for the three of us. Instead we were seven, including a baby, part of a panicked group fleeing Europe. But my memories are panic free. For me, the voyage was an adventure. My most exotic treat was having a slice of apple pie, à la mode.

How did my mother decide what to leave in the Zürich apartment and what to pack for America, knowing she would never see her possessions again? Why did she bring two brick-hard green silk pillows that took up lots of space? They were uncomfortable. They had no use. Possibly the tiny pink rose pattern reminded her of the sofas and chairs she had to leave behind. Why not more silver, or dishes? She rolled up the Gobelin tapestry with its scene of Versailles but left the broad gilt frame behind. She must have been advised not to take it, too heavy, too expensive. She could always buy a new frame in America. Now the Gobelin hangs in our guest bedroom at Wake Robin without a frame. The pillows are gone, but the tapestry remains, a reminder of the comfortable middle-class life my mother once had. Some stitches have frayed and the fabric needs to be cleaned, but the elegant couple still dances in the courtyard. He takes a deep bow in a heavy blue cape; she is entranced, dressed in a pink silk gown. I dreamt about them as a child.

MY MOTHER EXPERIENCED only two financial phases: upper middle-class comfort when she was married to my successful businessman father, and financial uncertainty at the age of thirty-six when my father committed suicide. Each year, as her income grew less, her anxiety grew more. Still, she went to the beauty parlor on schedule, if not once a week, then once every two weeks, and smoothed Elizabeth Arden on her face every other night.

A manicure was more of a luxury for my mother than it is for me. We were not poor, but we were very careful. I now understand that there was no backup plan to support us. She alone was responsible for her family, and so she counted every penny. From her I learned to save. I would pile up the dollar bills and stack the quarters high after each day waiting on tables at Chef Karl's in Lenox where I worked every summer while in college. Those quarters and dollar bills paid for my room, board, and tuition; there were no college loans.

I began to relax about money when I got married.

Then my old anxiety about money returned when I was newly divorced. I fantasized about stealing a roll of toilet paper from a public restroom, but never did. Too bulky. I sank comfortably back into the pillow of economic security when I remarried. I've had to unlearn much of what she taught me about money—that we had to be very thrifty, that there would never be quite enough. Still, when I get my nails done I feel like I'm indulging in a small luxury. I can file my own nails well enough. Clear polish does not really require expertise. The manicure makes me feel good, clean, and more beautiful. My nails advertise who I am: a woman who takes the time to take good care of herself. I like the feeling I have when the manicurist holds my pliant hand in hers like a tray and pays full attention to each of my fingers, one by one, until every cuticle is pushed back and every nail glistens evenly. She removes any mistakes with a knife-edged Kleenex, slicing away spills with the precision of a surgeon.

My mother was drawn to pink shades. I stick to neutral. Now and then I wear red nail polish, though it has to be a special occasion. My mother chose between two nail styles: a half moon, which leaves a half circle bare at the base, or polish on the entire nail. Both require precision, but the half-moons are more difficult, and therefore, more elegant. She did not want to look garish. She was a lady. Women made regular appointments then, for a manicure and wash and set. Hair was "set" in pin curls or rollers. The objective was control. My mother would sit under the beastly hot dryer with long silver clips pinching the sides of her head. They left even waves and created the illusion of a full head of hair.

My mother began to worry about her thinning hair when she was in her early sixties, like I worry now in my eighties. Her hair was thinner than mine, which should make me feel good. It was no thicker than strands of unspooled gray thread. Edgar, my brother, would look down on the top of her head from his great height and joke with her about becoming bald. He would stroke her scalp with his broad hand and add rough, teasing words. She was caught between laughter and distress; his attention felt good even if it hurt.

I laughed too, even when I shouldn't have. I hoped that my mother would not raise the hand mirror to reflect the baby-pink patches on her head. I do not raise my mirror either. A frontal view is best. My hairdresser, Steve, does such a good job of puffing my hair into a white crown he then sprays in place. When I look in the mirror, I see that my hair has become a deflated

Governor Ann Richards. I would not get older like my mother did, I told myself when I was young. But I ask my hairdresser the same question my mother must have asked: "Is my hair getting thinner?" Neither of us would have wanted an honest answer, and I never get one.

"I keep finding gray hairs on the back of my sweater," I sigh.

"Some will grow back," Steve assures me. And I believe him, until I find the next few hairs settled down on my black wool dress like silky lint. My husband picks them off and hands them to me between his thumb and second finger, like some specimen. I shrug.

ꝯ December 21, 2016

I made my bed this morning,
wanting to get back in.
The white duvet won't
stay flat like it should
at seven in the morning.
Puffiness beckons
me to lie supine
as white light
sinks me into sinful
repose, devoid
of dreams
and things to do
and places to be
on the dot of time.
Why not live back to front
and enjoy the best part
of the closing day in the morning.
When lavender drops
fall on my pillow,
and my feet find heat
at the foot of the bed.

I prop my head
and coax the light to
my open book, I want
so much to finish,
before I disappear.
from myself.
I would have to be sick
or dead
to get permission
to smooth the covers
sweetly over my body
in daylight.
I dare not ask,
not yet, not yet.

8

Downsizing

ॐ

I HARBOR A SENTIMENTAL LONGING FOR A HOME-
STEAD, a place where each generation has written
their births and deaths in the family bible kept in
a safe place. But World War II scattered us about, to
England, to Israel, and to America in search of safety.
That is why I cannot dispose of my mother's good
white tablecloths with matching initialed napkins or
get rid of Aunt Berthe's Rosenthal gold-edged teacups
and flowered dessert plates. *They* are my past.

As I pack them up, I carefully hold a cup in my
hand and examine the painted rose scene on its side.
Why do I not use my "good" dishes? What am I saving

them for? I vow that I will use them at Wake Robin, a place where private dinner parties no longer happen. And, when John and I eat dinner at home, I will take out two of the white-gold rimmed dishes my first husband and I carefully selected before our wedding. My mother's good silver will come out too, whether it's polished or not.

I walk through the condo and survey the magnitude of the moving job ahead—books and more books, boxes and boxes of stored papers, stacks of writings that someday might be discovered by one of my children and assembled into another book or provide material for an historian. Photographs of the children, of me with dignitaries, of me at various stages of my public life: fly fishing, signing bills, tapping the first maple tree, standing in the center of a group of women, of a group of children, of a group of men.

Boxes are everywhere. In the garage, they are stacked up to the ceiling, already sagging with the weight of time. Each box demands a decision: keep, toss, or re-box when I am too exhausted to decide. Metal shelves hold paintings and posters and framed awards that are not good enough to hang on the wall, but not bad enough to discard. It seems an unforgivable discourtesy to throw an award into the trash and lose those words of precious praise. I fill five boxes of them (tossing in glass candy dishes, vases, bowls, and small clocks, all embossed with my title and name) and label them to go to the University of Vermont. I won't have to think about them any further. If they are relegated to the library basement, I will never know.

I ask my son and daughter-in-law to take the glass lamps and the carved ivory depiction of the signing of the Magna Carta. My other son looks through the boxes of books and I say, "Take what you want." My stepdaughter brings home the white fleece sheep rocker that my grandchildren loved to sit on. Now it goes to her grandchildren. I have an inward battle. I am glad to see these possessions taken away; I have to free myself of space-consuming pieces. And yet, I want to weep. I had only begun to love them.

The books are the hardest to sort out. I had been thrilled to read the *Alexandria Quartet* by Lawrence Durrell, which everyone was talking about in the 1970s. I stepped into the lives of unfaithful friends described by John Updike. I was intrigued by the inner lives of Philip Roth's male characters. I fell in love with Anita Brookner's lonely women and wrote her a fan letter to which she replied. Margaret Atwood and Alice Munro felt like friends. If I simply perused the covers, would that give me enough nostalgic pleasure to justify keeping them on the shelf? When a few of them are resettled at Wake Robin, I enjoy looking at them. It is enough.

While packing I discover a small, thin, faded-blue paperback wedged between two pushy hardcovered books. I carefully pull it out. The pages are edged in brown. It has become old like me. The signs of wear surprise me; I had not expected stationary books to age in place. I read the title: *Evangeline and Other Poems*, copyright 1946. In pencil on the inside cover I have written "Madeleine May, 8A1" (eighth grade, P.S. 101). I recite the opening lines. "This is the forest primeval, the murmuring pines and the hemlocks."

Do I keep it or give it away? Would the library even take it? I hold on to it, knowing I am not likely to reread it but reminded of smelly navy-blue gym uniforms, the steel jungle gyms, my old lunch box. And oh, yes, Miss Lutz, the spinster principal who towered over us. I place *Evangeline* where I can see her, next to my computer.

The closets are scrunched with clothes from four seasons and several lifetimes. I am not ready to give away the expensive silk suit I wore at Peter and Lisa's wedding twenty-three years ago. I have worn it only once since the wedding, but still, it cost so much it has to stay. The same thinking prevents me from disposing of the ice blue silk suit I wore for my swearing in as ambassador to Switzerland. I was pleased that my elegant attire could equal the ornate, gold-trimmed room of the State Department. I have a photo of me and Madeleine Albright, who officiated. I take each suit out of the closet, one at a time, give them a final, tender look, and mercilessly squash them into the black plastic trash bag. I pull the red plastic ribbons tight. They may have another life, I console myself, thinking of their happy rediscovery.

The three formal gowns from each of my inaugural balls are stored in the downstairs coat closet, off to one side, safe in their hermetically sealed and zippered bags. I designed them myself and an Austrian dressmaker made them. At my first ball I wore a maroon velvet gown with large puffy sleeves, a narrow waist, and a full skirt—a medieval princess leaning out of the tower. I asked the seamstress to copy the second gown from a Lord & Taylor advertisement in the *New York Times*, a slim black velvet gown with a broad white satin shawl collar. For my third, a fitted navy blue velvet top and a full, shiny, taffeta skirt. Should I try them on before zipping them up again? No. It doesn't seem right to expose myself to certain disappointment. I know the zippers won't go all the way up, not only because I have gained weight (not too much), but also because the shape of my body has changed, particularly from the waist down. It feels like bad luck to put them on again. Each gown is like a wedding dress: to be worn only once.

I have to save them. They belong to history; this is what the first female governor of Vermont wore at her inaugural ball. I consider calling the Vermont Historical Society to ask if they will store them. The thought of the gowns displayed on mannequins, who look perpetually young, is pleasing. The gowns will continue to be who I once was. As with many such ideas, I never follow up. Instead, I ask the moving company to provide a tall cardboard clothing box that I place in storage cage number eighteen in the basement at Wake Robin for twenty dollars a month. It seems worth it.

So much of what we decide to keep is built on "someday." Someday we might need it; someday we would wish we had kept it. Someday is shorter than it used to be. The word itself has shrunk. If someday hasn't happened by now, I have to accept that it is not likely that it will. If I haven't looked through my library of big, beautiful art books in the last ten years, I probably won't take them down from the shelf in the next five, or in whatever time I have left. If I haven't sorted through the boxes of photographs, still in the envelopes they came in when I picked them up from the photography section of the drugstore, I am not about to cull them now. But someday itself is hard to discard. I still cling to the belief that someday, I will have empty hours to happily sort through my boxes of photographs. For now, I reach up and plunk the sagging boxes down on the top shelf of the garage.

Some things no one wants but I can't give away. I have two silver tea sets. One belonged to my mother and the other to Aunt Berthe. Every middle-class European bride once was given such a set as a wedding present. My mother once confessed to me, with an unusual note of jealousy in her voice, that her older sister Berthe's set was genuine silver, while hers was plated. I can see my Aunt Berthe slowly pouring from it, careful not to spill a drop on the crisp, white-stitched tablecloth, mixing the desired amount of tea with hot water, strong or weak. Now both sets are more black than silver, as if in mourning for their neglect. I have my excuses. For some years after I inherited my mother's set I polished it, not as well as my mother or a housekeeper might have done, but well enough to find a place for it on the dining room buffet. Then I stopped polishing and it was kept in the dark. That is how it ended up in the laundry room hidden behind the door and on top of an old sewing machine. It deserves better. My mother would be dismayed. She had insisted on including the tea set among the few possessions she packed to come to America. It, like us, was a refugee, a reminder of comfortable middle-class life. As I place the tarnished silver lid back on the sugar bowl, I turn to my son Daniel with a question: "Will you take it?" He agrees.

My daughter-in-law Jane says she doesn't want any of our possessions. She and Adam are regularly carting their own things off to the Goodwill. Clutter has already become their enemy. How wise. If only we had done that earlier, then I would not be faced with disposing half a lifetime of possessions, each with its own archaeological history. The right time to denude the condo would have been before we moved into Wake Robin, a year and a half ago. But I was not yet ready to let go and adhered to the illusion that we did not really live at Wake Robin. I wanted our home to continue to be where it had been for the last ten years: 9 Harbor Watch. That was where we had been young, well, and happy. At Wake Robin, we would be old.

Setting a date for the sale of the condo felt cruel. Tearing home apart feels like pulling off a spider's legs, one at a time. It's an autopsy of space—once alive, now dead. But I knew it had to be done, for John, for my stepdaughter, and, however reluctantly, for my own sake. I couldn't continue to long for the condo while living at Wake Robin, and John had begun to obsess over the need to sell it. These worries woke him up at two in the morning and wouldn't let him go back to sleep until the next day. He wanted things settled. He asked himself repeatedly, what would happen to the condo if he died before it was sold? Would I be able to afford the expense of keeping it? The condo became a constant irritant that rubbed him raw. Selling it would be the best ointment.

MY POSSESSIONS ARE MOVED out in separate brigades. Three cars and six Burlington library volunteers arrive on schedule one morning to take away all the boxed books. First Adam and then Daniel help me bring things to the synagogue. Peter brings things to the Goodwill. My friends Nancy and Peter distribute five filing cabinets and a set of bookcases. I arrange for a rug, art books, and a coffee table to be brought to my daughter, Julia, in Brooklyn. The owner of a secondhand furniture store, from whom we bought the dining room table for Wake Robin, comes and decides which pieces to take back on consignment. Slowly, the condo undresses itself. I call "1-800-Junk."

"We take anything," the man on the phone says.

"Anything?" I repeat.

"Anything."

Two medium-sized trucks pull in and stop in front of the garage. I give them everything that is left: flower pots, rakes, old pictures, old pots and pans.

"You sure you want to give us this?" One of the men is holding up a plaster flamenco figure I made when I was taking a sculpture class as a new bride.

I am ruthless. "Yes, take it. Take it, take everything," I repeat, feeling a sudden surge of fierce happiness.

The driver is having a great time. He finds a silver wig in the trash pile and puts it on. One Halloween I wore it for fun at a staff meeting in the Department of Education. He finds another treasure, a gold cardboard crown studded with glass diamonds, and balances it on top of the sparkling wig. He waves to me from inside the truck, one leg hooked over the wooden side panel. He looks hilarious. I laugh and wave back.

Before he leaves, he takes a wide broom and sweeps the entire garage. I feel cleansed, liberated, light. It is over.

Learning to walk at Aunt Berthe's house in Switzerland.

My parents, Ferdinand and Renée.

Me and Edgar, four years apart.

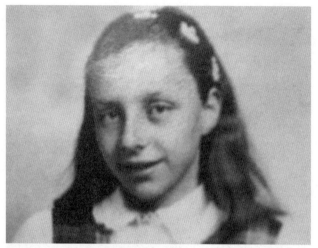

Me, eleven years old.

College graduation photo, University of Massachusetts, Amherst.

First legislative race photo.

At the governor's desk with Edgar.

End of 3rd term photo.

Cutting a ribbon.

Greeting a little girl.

Me and Rosalind Carter.

President Reagan and First Lady Nancy.

Campaigning with Geraldine Ferraro, 1984, Burlington.

With the First Lady and President Bush.

To Madeleine with gratitude that you ventured onto the slopes with me — Your friend, Hillary

Me and Hillary at Davos, Switzerland.

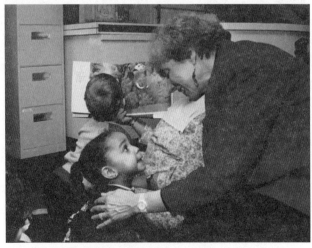

Department of Education visiting kindergarten.

With the Clinton team.

Throwing out the first ball on Vermont Day at Fenway, Boston.

With President Obama.

The Family: Peter, Adam, Daniel, Arthur, and Julia.

*At the Women's March
in Montpelier.*

With the Emerge Vermont class of 2018.

Me and John.

ℰ I Am Multiples

The dancer's
elastic poses
stretch my legs
high and wide
air up, I fall
on his raised hand
as if nothing
had happened.

The opera singer sways
my sucking ribs.
Her high octaves
tremble my bones
and wrinkle my throat
as I spill
gallons of sound
all over myself.

I'm on the tennis court
with someone else's arm,
Venus or Serena?

My body obeys
every quick command
from head to foot.
Look.
Just inside the line
by half an inch,
the camera assents.

The cello is settled between
bent legs, and curved arms
leaving fingers free to run
up and down, in
pursuit of fleeing notes
that I gulp down
into a thick, low sound
that feels good inside.

I abscond with the poet's words
and claim them for my own.
Or were they mine,
in the beginning?
I mouth them
with tongue and teeth,
and spit them in your face.

The writer says what I
wish to say,
leading me from
room to room in her house,
which seems eerily familiar.
She lived there once.

Chisel, brush, pen
bare faced, fully awake
ready for action.
Move, they say, like
we did, and make a mark.
I do, asking Monet, Manet
and ninety-year-old Picasso
to leave me a space.

I am multiples
and I am none.
It is late,
it is done.

9

Finding a Seat

꽃

I LOOK FOR THE RESTROOM before I sit down in a restaurant or take my seat in a theatre. I try to leave quickly at intermission to get at the head of the line in order to make it back before the second act begins. Bathrooms have become familiar places.

I appreciate a clean one, abhor a dirty one. When I use a public toilet, I sometimes forget to wipe the seat before I sit down. My mother always did. She thought that a swipe of toilet paper eliminated germs. I know better, and do it not for the germs, but for the urine. I feel sullied and offended when I feel someone else's droplets on my buttocks. There is a silent agreement that we women make: you leave the seat dry for me, and I leave it the same for you.

At the Flynn theatre in Burlington, I sometimes see a line in front of the men's room. The men look awkward, embarrassed. We women are used to lines. The public portrayal of an urgent physical need does not bother us. When a stall door opens up, I walk quickly to it before anyone else does. I feel triumphant. It's my space.

The line in front of the ladies' room can be a good place to have a conversation, usually centered on complaining about the long lines for the ladies' room. I have, once or twice, when I thought no one was looking and the concert was about to begin, darted into the men's room. Once it was accidental and a startled man turned around. "I never thought I'd meet the governor here." Another time it was on purpose. I was in a hurry. The men's room is a different world. It smells of men.

When I close the toilet door, I am in my private space, if only for three minutes. That is one advantage women have over men: we can close the door every time. American toilets leave open space above and below the door, possibly to enable us to climb over or under the door in an emergency, though I have never seen anyone do this. European toilets are like small rooms, totally enclosed. I like the feeling of being alone in a bathroom stall. It provides respite from the chaotic world beyond. I recapture my equilibrium there. I relax. The ladies' room is a safe space. It can be a place to go to cry.

❦

I WAS AT MY FIRST MEETING of the powerful Joint Fiscal Committee, the money committees of the House and Senate. It was 1978. No sooner had I taken my seat at the table than nominations for officers were made and accepted in rapid order: click, click. My delight caught in my throat. What had I missed? There must have been a meeting before the meeting, possibly in the men's room.

"I nominate Mrs. Kunin for secretary," Representative Peter Giuliani announced.

"I decline," I responded. I was certain that I did not want to slip into that "female" slot.

Representative Giuliani decided to be funny. "I say, let's make Mrs. Kunin chair of the Entertainment Committee."

They laughed.

I seethed.

My blood rose to my cheeks like mercury in a thermometer. They are mocking me. I am not being taken seriously. I'm here to entertain the men, like a play-thing, or worse. It's my fault. The pressure behind my eyes became stronger. Please, don't let me cry.

And so I sat grim-faced through the end of the meeting. When it was over I got up and rushed down the hall, turning neither left or right, and ran into the ladies' room, into a stall, and cried. When I felt ready to face the world, I washed my hands and told my story to the woman at the next sink. I didn't know her. She listened. I felt better.

This past year I saw a newspaper photo of the newly appointed Joint Fiscal Committee. All four members were women.

ℰ Teeth

I spit them out like olive pits,
tainted yellow and hard,
uprooted from the cave
of my cheek, where my
tongue fingers empty rooms.
I contort my smile
to hide the hag
I have become.
My tongue takes
measurements
in and out,
back and forth.
My lids seek light
I open wide,
one tooth hanging
on the edge of a cliff,
another set in a tub of space
where it may wobble
and loose balance.

I panic at the thought.
I must bare my teeth
in self-defense.
I must chomp my way
into old age.
Ah, I smile
and open wide
and lift my electric toothbrush
off of its solid base,
and brush and brush
and brush.

10

Alone

❦

THE STATE DEPARTMENT PERMITS new ambassadors to travel first class on their inaugural voyage to posts, and so I had a good night's sleep on Swiss Air, stretching out completely under a cloud-soft duvet. When the sun came up and the plane door opened, I was greeted by Michael Polt, the deputy chief of mission who had served as ambassador in the interim between the previous ambassador and myself. My cousin Irene was there too, and we embraced. Irene and Michael each handed me a large and glorious bouquet of flowers.

The ambassador's residence in Bern would be my home, but not mine alone. It had been furnished over many years by the State Department and by faceless previous ambassadors, and it would continue to serve as a public space. I would share it with countless visitors, as well as the butler, the maids, the gardener, and the chef.

The first thing I did after arriving was to remove the dusty, leather-bound books from the shelves in one of the two adjoining living rooms. A brown smell rose up; they had been untouched for a long time and were more like wallpaper than books. They seemed sad. No one had opened them in years. I stashed them in boxes and the butler relegated them to the basement. Instead, I filled the shelves with my favorite books with their gaudy covers and uneven sizes—a full set of Updike, Phillip Roth, Sylvia Plath, Kurt Vonnegut, and the almost complete works of Anita Brookner.

I felt, with a self-conscious pride, that I was revealing an important part of myself. The inventory was personal. Most intimate were the thin books of poetry I had acquired over a lifetime, some with covers that had begun to show their age. I wanted the guests to know who I was and also wished to provide an overview of American literature. In my more self-congratulatory moments, I believed my books would demonstrate that I was well-read. To be *kultiviert* earns more status in Europe than in the United States.

Then I unpacked photographs of my grandparents and my father and mother and placed them on an oblong table in the hallway. I wanted them there with me in the residence. They were part of the story. I placed my grandfather's portrait next to my father's. Both were tinted sepia brown, taken by the same photographer on the same day. My father holds a folded newspaper on his lap. His back is as straight as a soldier's.

Through the Arts in Embassies program, the State Department allowed me to select my own paintings and sculpture for the residence, limited only by the generosity of museums and private collections. The day the works of art arrived and were unwrapped was one of my happiest. The walls would now reflect my taste, and I would be warmed by their company. I replaced the china plates in the dining room vitrine with jolly circus figures lent by Vermont's Shelburne Museum. I wanted to give my guests objects that would elicit delight and prompt conversation.

The Arts in Embassies program is designed to function as soft diplomacy. I had hoped that my books would have the same effect, but their impact was subtle.

I rarely heard a comment. Only two or three people commented on the Faulkner and Joyce volumes on my shelves. Most gave the shelves a languid overview, wine glass in hand, while searching for someone to talk to.

As ambassador, my residence was an attractive venue for diplomatic discussions with Swiss parliamentarians and government officials. I was frequently invited to dinner parties at people's homes because of my status as the American ambassador, and I had the enormous benefit of being able to return invitations to dine at my own residence without lifting a finger. After breakfast, I would sit down with the chef and plan menus. Just before people arrived for dinner, I would survey the dining room table: ornate silver candlesticks, beautiful flower arrangements, sparkling silverware, and the official gold-rimmed china with its eagle crest. I was ready to be the host.

The subject of our diplomatic discussions, for almost my entire stay, was the role of neutral Switzerland during World War II when it was surrounded by Nazi occupied countries. The United States, under pressure from aging Holocaust survivors, was demanding that dormant Swiss bank accounts (accounts whose owner could not be found) be identified and returned to the heirs of the survivors or victims. The Swiss were adhering to their normal bureaucratic procedures and made no exceptions as they asked for death certificates from relatives of concentration camp victims. It was as if they were oblivious to the horror beyond their borders.

The spotlight was on the Swiss banks. In an effort to be transparent, they published a list of dormant account holders. While skimming the list in the *Financial Times* one morning, I saw a name: Renée May. My mother. They could have found her if they had tried. They could have found me. Was the same true of the other names? I kept these thoughts to myself.

"Did Bill Clinton appoint you to be the ambassador because you're Jewish?" I was asked.

"Of course not. He probably doesn't even know," I replied.

Almost every day, I met or spoke with a banking or government official, or members of the international Jewish community. One morning I visited Herr Meyer, the head of the Swiss banking association, whose office was on the top floor of Bank Sarasin in Basel. The banks had found a mere handful of accounts by then, and I described the power imbalance between the banks and the Holocaust survivor or heir: there was a long form to fill out, and then a hefty sum to the banks to conduct a search, and that was only the beginning.

Meyer was on the defensive. There was no need to do anything. Very few Jews deposited their fortunes in Swiss banks; instead, they would send money to America, he explained. I tried to pierce his official position, but I failed.

I took the elevator down the eight floors to the lobby and was greeted, for the first time, by my French cousin. Germaine Molina had written me a letter when I arrived at the embassy and invited me to have lunch. We hugged for a long minute. As we walked down the street to her favorite Italian restaurant, I described my conversation with Meyer. Suddenly, tears ran down my cheeks. I could not stop.

When we sat down to eat, Germaine started telling me family stories. Cousin Andre and his wife, Mimi, were interned in a Swiss refugee camp. Andre's brother was arrested in Paris and never seen again. Others were turned back at the border, only to fall into the hands of the Nazis. If only Herr Meyer could have seen their faces. Would he have understood? If only I could have made their case more effectively.

A conservative parliamentarian, Adolphe Blöcher, made a statement: "All the Jews want is money." I winced. No, the search for the thousands of bank accounts was about the thousands of people who had died. The banks could not be allowed to make them disappear again.

I felt a deep responsibility. I carried it daily as I praised Swiss parliamentarians for inaugurating a study of Switzerland's role during World War II and criticized the banks for stonewalling. I played good cop, bad cop. It took a toll on me emotionally when I had to control my frustration, even anger. There were few outlets.

But my books served me well. I took out a volume or two quite often after the parties had ended and I found myself alone with that special loneliness that follows all goodbyes. I had come to Bern soon after my divorce from the man who was the father of our four children, and to whom I had been married for thirty-seven years. I did not have a partner. I felt the vacuum, especially when everyone had left and I was alone in a way I never had been before.

My previous presidential appointment had been as deputy secretary of education in Washington. I had been separated from my husband for much of that time but hadn't experienced the same loneliness that I experienced in Switzerland. In Washington, I first had a small apartment on Porter Street, and then moved in with two housemates to Ordway Street. Any sign of loneliness was quickly dispelled by our shared conversations over breakfast or after work. We were three lonely women who pretended not be. And we had jobs.

Life in Washington taught me how to maneuver in social situations. I could walk into a cocktail reception by myself with a straight back and a forced smile. I would pause at the entrance, as uncoupled people do, and look around. The advantage of being single in Washington was that there were many single women in the city, some of whom held powerful government positions. They were interesting to talk to and they could extend a lot of useful information. It was easy to join such a cluster and have a good time without a man.

One August weekend, the air was thick with heat and no matter how hard I tried to rid myself of the teenage fear of facing a Saturday night alone, I could not succeed. I had bought a nice piece of salmon, one potato, greens for a salad, and a proper bottle of white wine at the grocery store on Connecticut Avenue. My plastic bag was digging into my hand as I walked slowly home down the hill on Porter Street. I was hot. For no obvious reason, I started to cry. No one saw me.

I asked myself, would I ever find love again? I had dated several men in Washington, but no one seriously. I had begun to feel that a powerful woman sets off a flashing yellow light to prospective male companions: caution, she may be too much for you. Accomplished as Washington women may be, the power apex remains male. Or a man might call me out of curiosity, wondering what it would be like to go out with a former governor. When I was in office in Vermont, men did not hesitate to kiss me on the cheek and remark, chuckling, "I never kissed a Governor before."

In my job, at least, I was hardly ever alone. The US Department of Education employed three thousand people, and when I was on official travel, a staff person always accompanied me. I became close with the three women who reported directly to me, and they took me on a shopping trip to several discount department stores to buy formal wear for my new life in Switzerland. I tried on sequined gowns and satin dresses, both long and short. We had a wonderful time.

"That one is perfect."

"No, that one."

"I'll take them both, the price is right." And we all laughed. I felt elegant, svelte, and exactly like an ambassador.

In Switzerland, my social life was different. It was more difficult to make friends with other single women, and I soon learned that the Swiss concept of elegance is not formal wear, but rather a well-tailored suit made with expensive fabric and elegant buttons. I took my formal gowns off their hangers in the huge closets of my residence only twice a year, the first for the annual Marine Ball, a festive event held in the spring at every American embassy. The first year, I invited the French ambassador to escort me. I danced and sparkled happily. At the subsequent Marine Balls, he was not available, and I knew no other single men to ask. I would dance one dance with a very polite, elegantly uniformed Marine and leave early, drained of energy by my efforts to be sociable and to pretend that I was not embarrassed by being single.

At night, I often passed by my books and family photos on my way upstairs. I said goodnight to them before I mounted the curved staircase to my bedroom where the covers were already pulled back by the maid. For those three years, I never had to make a bed, shop for food, do laundry, cook, dust a photograph, wash the dishes, or set the table. Or drive. Vernon would appear at the front door with his spotless Lincoln Town car to take me wherever I needed to go, wait there until

I was ready to leave, and then bring me home. It was a wonderful life, in almost every respect. But as I got undressed and into bed, I would wonder what time it was in America.

❦ Autumn

I would like to know the secret
of the dull brown oak leaves
that hold on and hold on
to the black branches.
I watch them sway every which way
in gusts that follow
one another.
I see one fall, but it is
only a leaf swept up from the
ground and tossed as if
it were still alive.

11

Independence

ɕ

M Y BROTHER EDGAR voted for Eisenhower, I for Adlai Stevenson. I could not understand his reasoning. But I fell in love with Stevenson's use of language and a little bit with him. We had met when he and his two sons and his entourage visited the Brussels World's Fair. Carol Hardin, his first cousin and my roommate, was his host. When we walked down the street in Brussels and encountered two GIs, he pushed his hand forward and said, "Hiya soldier, where you from?" The start of a conversation. I sat in the back of the room when he held a press conference and was enraptured by his deft responses and clear language. But my only reaction to what I was witnessing was to think that someday, I might like to be married to a politician. I realized later, as Gloria Steinem said, that "we have become the men we wanted to marry."

After I returned from the Brussels World's Fair, Edgar and I decided to spend a ski weekend at a lodge in Stowe. At the time, my love life was complicated. I was still in love with Dale, my classmate at the Columbia School of Journalism, who my mother disapproved of for reasons that now seem secondary: Dale was not Jewish. Then, in Burlington, where I had taken my first reporting job at the *Burlington Free Press*, I met Arthur. He was an ideal husband—a doctor, Jewish, smart, and kind—whereas Dale's future was unclear and he was not ready to ask me to marry him.

I observed Edgar at the ski lodge. He attracted women with his easy charm and movie star looks, and he enjoyed being a practiced flirt. But to me, the women seemed needy and sad even though they could not have been much older than I was, in their mid to late twenties. They looked old and I hated the game they were playing. I made a decision. I never wanted to embarrass myself to get a man. I would not place myself in that position. I would marry the man who would take me out of the hunt and make me (and incidentally, my mother) happy.

When I was a senior at the University of Massachusetts in Amherst, I was awarded a thousand-dollar scholarship from the Massachusetts Women's Clubs to do graduate work anywhere. I had been accepted at the Columbia University School of Journalism and at the London School of Economics. My German professor proposed that I attend the London School, but my mother did not want me to go to Europe and leave her alone in her apartment in Pittsfield. I felt the responsibility to compensate for my father's death and take care of my mother, but the urge to follow my professor's advice was equally strong. Studying in London would be an adventure.

Edgar sided with my mother. After graduating from Columbia, he told me, I could get a job, while the London School would lead nowhere. (Neither of us knew what a rich intellectual climate it would have provided.) I did not have the will to fight back. I obeyed and enrolled at Columbia, only to learn a month later that Edgar would be traveling throughout Europe with his friend Bob. He had not asked for permission.

I understood then that I had to emancipate myself from my brother's influence if I were to become the person I wanted to be, even before I knew who that person was. I wanted to do what he could do, without losing my mother's love. The perfect combination would have been to be become both the good daughter and the strong son. Good enough to stay, strong enough to leave.

I realize now that Edgar also had to distinguish himself from me. This became apparent when I was elected governor. He was a man; he was four years older; he should have been able to go first. He had been first when he was awarded a Pulitzer Prize in journalism. This was the same year that my first baby, Julia, was born. When my mother, brother, husband, and I met in a Rutland secondhand bookstore (midway between our home in Burlington and my mother's in Pittsfield) to celebrate, I held out five-month-old Julia for my mother's admiration and Edgar held out his Pulitzer Prize. That day my ambition was limited to finding a place where I could breastfeed the baby. Public breastfeeding would have been considered indecent in 1961, and so the bookstore owner led me to a back room where I wouldn't be disturbed.

I EXPERIENCED THE FIRST STIRRINGS of political desire in Switzerland, during Arthur's sabbatical year at the University of Bern. I had left behind me a part-time job teaching freshman English at Trinity College in Burlington, staying up past midnight correcting 150 papers from three classes and nursing a new baby. I looked forward to a year in Switzerland as a wife and mother.

It was 1971, the year that Swiss women were pressing for the right to vote, and I watched the televised debates and felt I was watching a replay of the American suffrage movement. American women had gained the right to vote fifty-one years earlier but still had not achieved what Swiss women were asking for: gender equality. Their arguments thrilled me. I decided that when we returned to the United States, I would get involved in the feminist movement.

Meanwhile, I immersed myself in the new feminist literature: *The Second Sex*, by Simone de Beauvoir, *The Feminine Mystique*, by Betty Friedan, *Sexual Politics*, by Kate Millett, *The Female Eunuch*, by Germaine Greer, and *Sisterhood is Powerful*, edited by Robin Morgan. I celebrated their messages. At last, someone was saying what I had been thinking. I was not alone in my rebellion against the social norm for doctors' wives, which often required a woman to work to put her husband through medical school. Her happiness, status, and pride were all derived from being a doctor's wife, not any achievement of her own. In Switzerland, the spouse of a PhD or a physician was called Frau Doktor, and if he was also a professor, like my husband, she was greeted as "Frau Doktor Professor." I took the feminist call to action personally. It changed my timetable. I could reenter the world beyond domesticity. I had thought I would wait to pursue my life's ambitions until I had completed the responsibilities of motherhood, when my children would be safely ensconced in college. That sabbatical year became a year of thinking. Yes, I would somehow do it all.

As an immigrant child, I was shaped by my mother's courage and resilience. Her story has grown larger as I have grown older. I wanted to be different from her and her accent. I wanted to be like everybody else, to be part of a real American family that served peanut butter and jelly sandwiches with the crusts neatly cut off for lunch. I did not want to be part of an odd-numbered threesome: me, my brother, and mother. I wanted to belong, to be an insider, not an outsider. There is no faster road to insider status than being elected to public office. As a representative, I would be part of them; I would be we.

I turned to Edgar again as I debated whether to run

for a seat in the Vermont House of Representatives. Edgar urged me to wait. Ronald Reagan would be on the presidential ballot; it was not a good time to run as a Democrat. I turned to another mentor, Vic Maerki, who had been a senior reporter when I was at the *Burlington Free Press*. Vic urged me to run. I agreed. My regret about not going to the London School of Economics may have prompted my decision.

I campaigned every evening after supper, leaving the dishes to my husband to go out and knock on neighbors' doors. Arthur was highly supportive. His backing gave me courage. Sometimes I brought my oldest children, then ten and twelve, with me. I enjoyed the doorway conversations, the challenge of making connections with strangers. On election night, we celebrated my success in our living room.

One year later, Edgar and his wife, Judith, returned to his home in Springfield, Vermont, from Paris, where he had been an assistant to Ambassador Sargent Shriver. There they established themselves quickly enough for Edgar to run for the Vermont House of Representatives as a Democrat. His victory marked the beginning of the end of Republican domination in the town and eventually, in the county. I was happy with the coincidence that we would both serve in the legislature, but also harbored an unpleasant nagging feeling that my brother would overshadow me with his eloquence. But I admired him greatly. When Edgar entered a room, he took up a big space, edging others into the corner. His generous shock of hair, penetrating blue eyes, tall stature, and a voice that carried drew all eyes to him. He argued well and held his position with a firm grip. And so I developed muscles of my own. By then I had been appointed to a seat on the House Appropriations Committee, seldom referred to without the anteced-ent "powerful" because it determined the budget. Edgar was on the Health and Welfare Committee. He immediately understood the power structure. Any bill that called for any dollar amount had to be approved by my committee. The tables turned when I became Governor and he was appointed chair of the Senate Appropriations committee.

I WAS A SHY CHILD. I am not sure how I learned to take the risk of running for office and exposing myself to the potential humiliation of defeat. To explain that I was propelled by my inner voice is too simple. But that is what happened when I gave my first speech to the House of Representatives. A Republican, Kenalene Collins, spoke against the ratification of the Equal

Rights Amendment. I could not bear to let her have the last word. I stood up and found my voice. My first victory. I made eye contact with the women sitting in the gallery watching the proceeding. We had campaigned for the Equal Rights Amendment together. I had spoken not only for myself, but for them. As we were filing out of the House, one curmudgeon of a legislator turned to me and said, "Just because you won your first one, don't think you're gonna win them all."

It was true. I lost my first campaign for governor in 1982. I was devastated. When I had announced that I would run for governor the year before, I was running for an open seat. Governor Richard Snelling had announced he was stepping down. But the next January, he changed his mind and decided to run for another term. I now faced a four-term incumbent and the race changed from one I was likely to win to one I was likely to lose. I did lose, but narrowly, which made my political career salvageable. Less than a year later, at ten o'clock in the morning, Governor Snelling announced again he would not seek another term. Five minutes later, I received a phone call.

"Really? Really? Are you sure?" was all I could say at first. "Let me think about it."

I thought it over for less than a day. Then I started making phone calls. I knew I could go down in history as a two-time loser, but I refused to dwell on that. I wanted to go down in history as a winner. That was worth the risk. I wanted, I confess, to make history. I wanted to be a role model, not only for other women, but also for my children. I wanted them to learn about resilience by seeing their mother spring back from defeat. On a deeper level, I had healed enough from the hurt of loss to try again

In 1995, I took the oath of governor. When Edgar escorted me down the center aisle of the House chamber to be sworn in, I held his arm tightly and we exchanged a brother-sister complicit smile. When Edgar was sworn into the Vermont Senate that same year, he requested the chairmanship of that powerful Senate Appropriations Committee. The governor proposes the budget and the legislature disposes, he would remind me. Before he was given the assignment, he had to assure the Senate leadership that he would not be his sister's lackey. He kept his word. He was chest-puffing proud of me. I was his sister.

❦ ANTS

I spared a spider her death
in the bathtub this morning.
She was doing no harm.
Let her live.
I get kinder as I get older,
more forgiving.
I step into the kitchen,
black ants crawling on the counter,
ants upside down on the walls.
My hand sweeps them to the floor,
quickly, not thinking,
I stomp on them
one by one by one.

12

Searching for the Past

ℰ

I'M INTERESTED IN FILLING in the blank spaces of my childhood. I want to know who my relatives were, how they lived, and how they died. I want the next generations to know where my family came from. I want to give them names, dates of birth, marriages, and deaths. And I want to extract my lost family from the anonymous six million killed in the Holocaust. How else am I to mourn them? Someone has to know; someone has to remember.

I am not a Holocaust survivor, but I harbor survivor's guilt. It was luck that spared us. My grandparents on my mother's side were French. They could have returned to their families just across the border from Basel, Switzerland, where they would likely have faced annihilation. My parents could have decided to live in Frankfurt, where my father had once lived and his shoe business was established. They could have moved to Ann Frank's Amsterdam, where my cousins Millie, Eric, and Yvonne lived and my father had an office. Instead, my parents settled in what turned out to be a safe haven: Zürich.

My parents, I now understand, had similar backgrounds, though my mother's family lived in France and my father's family in Germany. Both had lived in rural agricultural communities, the likely reason being that Jews were not permitted to reside in cities until they were emancipated by Napoleon. France was the second country, five hundred years after Poland, to grant Jews citizenship. This was in 1791. Other countries slowly followed. Switzerland waited until 1868, finally pressured by France and the United States to grant equal rights to Jews who were formerly restricted to the two small towns of Endingen and Langnau. When I made an official visit as ambassador to these towns on the occasion of the restoration of the synagogue, I noted that each house had two parallel entrances: one for Jews, and the other for Christians.

During my ambassadorship in Switzerland I met my daughter, Julia, in Wiesbaden, Germany, where she had a fellowship, and we traveled to my father's birthplace, a small farming village called Geinsheim, not far from Frankfurt. The officials in the town hall connected us to an unusual woman, Irmgard Schaffer, who had kept track of the Jews who had once lived there. When Julia and I sat at her dining room table and I brought up my father's name, she left the room and came back with a gray metal box filled with three-by-five index cards, like the ones I used to keep recipes. She pulled out a card: Ferdinand May. He had existed.

Mrs. Schaffer took us on a tour of the town, pointing out the street where my father went to the Jewish school, where my grandmother had her store, and the street where the Jews had lived. I asked her why she had so carefully documented the Jews who lived in Geinsheim. Her answer was simple. "When I was in school, two Jewish boys were singled out and made to stand in the back of the room. Then they couldn't attend school. I felt sorry for them." The boys had made the right decision and had gone to Israel. Mrs. Schaffer remained in touch with them.

On a street corner we encountered a man who asked us—we were obvious outsiders—what were we doing there? When we explained that we were looking for my father's family, he went back to his house and came back holding a book for me to keep. A photo of a group of people gathered around a table was on the cover. Were they celebrating a birthday, a holiday, or was it a dinner party? The title told the story: *Unsere verschwundenen Nachbarn (Our Disappeared Neighbors)*. I found my father's family name in the section about Geinsheim. They had traced the name May back to the seventeenth century. Was this where our name came from? Jews weren't allowed to have last names or citizenship until 1808.

The Jewish cemetery was located in the next town, Groß-Gerau. The cemetery, like all Jewish cemeteries in Germany, had been destroyed during Kristallnacht. This community had decided to restore it, and to identify and repair as many gravestones as possible. The cemetery keeper was proud of his work. He was the person I had been looking for, the "Good German." Within the cemetery's iron-gated walls, I found my grandfather's tombstone—Elias May. It was as if he had been waiting for me to arrive. Julia and I stood still and recited the Mourner's Kaddish together.

I then searched for evidence of my family in Alsace-Lorraine, France, as it was then called. My grandmother and grandfather had attended the same Hebrew school in Habsheim, taught by my grandfather's father, a rabbi. Jews had lived in these areas—many small villages in Alsace, now known for their wine and cuisine, had a "Rue des Juifs"—since the seventeenth century. Almost all are gone—left or been shipped to concentration camps. It is no coincidence that Alsace, which once contained the largest population of Jews in France, is now a stronghold for the National Front Party, a party known for its anti-Semitic and anti-immigrant policies.

I went to city hall to look for the names of my grandparents, Gaston Bloch and Aline Braunschweig. I expected difficulty—the name Bloch, I learned, was as common as Smith is in the United States—but was shocked when the clerk politely told me that the records had all been burned. So I continued my search in England, where most of my father's grandnieces and grandnephews lived. My father, the oldest of five children, made it possible for most of his family to leave Germany for England in the 1930s, all except one sister who, with her husband, died in Theresienstadt. I plied them with questions, but they were two generations removed from their immigrant grandparents and remembered little. My oldest cousin, Yvonne, born in Germany and who lives in London, was hidden in Holland during the war and moved from one hiding place to another. Her mother, Millie, was hidden elsewhere. "One family was nice," Yvonne recalled, and then she was moved to another family that wasn't.

Both mother and daughter survived, but Yvonne never recovered from the separation. She walks with a limp, a result of childhood polio. It has gotten worse as she has grown older. Yvonne contacted polio as a child and the doctor told her parents to hide her immediately because disabled children would be the first to be killed. Her father, who was sent to Auschwitz, sent a postcard home from the concentration camp, as if it were a resort, before he was exterminated.

Yvonne's mother lived to be 102. When I visited her with my son Daniel five years earlier, she looked at him and exclaimed, "Wie der Ferdinand, genau wie der Ferdinand!" (Like Ferdinand, exactly like Ferdinand). It was as if my father had walked into the room. Yvonne later came to visit me in Vermont and brought a family photo of herself with her parents, Millie and Erich Malekovski. In it she was about four years old. For years, I had imagined the story wrong. I thought she had been hidden as a baby; I had never imagined the three of them as a family, looking just

like any other family. She showed me another photograph taken in a garden. My father is stretched out
across my mother's lap on a bench. Both are laughing. I wish I knew the joke.

I do not remember my father's laugh, or his hands,
or his lap. I was two and a half years old when he
took his life. I am tempted to write "when he left."
My father left by rowboat on Lake Zürich and I imagine he jumped. After a week-long search, they never
found his body. As a young woman I imagined that
he had made it back to another shore and had gone
off to live a different life, that he would someday
come back, for me, for us.

My father was drafted into the German army
during World War I and had been gassed and left for
dead in the trenches. My mother believed that the
mustard gas had caused his depression. I now know
differently. It had to have been post-traumatic stress
disorder. The diagnoses, if correct, make it easier to
forgive him. He did not abandon me voluntarily.

My father's psychological wounds did not surface
until some years after he was rescued from the bat-
tlefield. He was hospitalized for depression twice at
a sanatorium in Kilchberg above Lake Zürich, now
called Klinik Im Park. I had wanted to visit, but when
I got the courage to do so, I was told by the voice

that answered the phone only relatives could visit. Relatives of the dead did not count.

I did receive part of his records, which confirmed his suicide. The day before he was to be released, my father rented a rowboat. He must have planned it carefully. Did he plunge from the boat, or did he slowly slip, knowing he would not be able to rise again and breathe? What was it like in the dark depths? Were his eyes open or closed? Could he have changed his mind midway? The face of death may have frightened him. He might have struggled then, desperate to lighten his weight, regretting that he could not swim.

When the news of his death reached us, I was too young to feel a thing. I think of him more now that I am older. Too old to have a father but not too old to mourn. I experience a different, darker grief for those who were murdered by the Nazis. The Holocaust killings are alive with horror. It is why they died and the way they died that compels me to pursue the past. My father was not a Holocaust victim. I understand that. But his death and the deaths of my family in the Holocaust blur together in my imagination.

I feel sorry for the guilt that my mother must have experienced. Against their recommendation, she had urged the doctors to let my father come home early for the national Swiss holiday on the first of August. She must have had plans for a picnic or a celebration. If, on the day before his discharge, my mother had taken one more walk with him on the green grounds of the sanitarium, or admired the view of the lake from above, would his suicide have been prevented? For a long time, she blamed herself for the hurt he had left for her on his bedside table. He thought it was a gift. "I am doing this for you."

I never thought that one day I would resemble my mother, trying to bring my husband out of his depression. John has no thoughts of suicide. At least, not yet. "I am doing this for you." I understand it better now, because those are the words that my husband says to me when he is suffering from depression and folds into himself.

"I don't want to burden you."

"Don't say that," I say. "Please." "

ℰ CHRISTMAS COOKIES

Swiss Christmas cookies,
you remembered
making them in our kitchen.
Why should that make me so happy?
Zimmet Sterne, Basler Leckerli,
Spitzbüben with raspberry jam.
You wanted to make some
with your brother in his kitchen.
My recipes were hard to read
smudged by bits of butter,
fingerprints of flour.
We went to the Internet and
found almost what we wanted.
The first batch failed because you
mistook powdered sugar for flour.
No wonder!
You turned red with laughter.
The next batch was perfect:
six-pointed stars with slivered
almonds on top.
You thought they should have been
darker, as you remembered.

But they were beautiful
and tasted just right.
I had been a good mother,
after all.

13

My Brother's Death

ঌ

AFTER MY ONLY BROTHER, EDGAR, died on December 27, 2012, I received a white, plastic-covered notebook with a copy of his green card on the cover and a draft of his memoir inside. Edgar had been working on his memoir off and on for about three years. From the start, he was secretive about it. He had kept the memoir from me while he was writing it, not having wanted me looking over his shoulder. He showed the first chapters to my husband, John, but not to me. Close as we were as siblings, our realities were individual, and I understood the contradiction between the desire to maintain privacy while writing a memoir and the urge to share it with the world when it was done.

Edgar wanted his legacy written in his words and found that writing about himself was easy compared to his early journalistic career. He had started writing his memoir when I began my last book, *The New Feminist Agenda*, and in the last year, he had written daily, giving me reports of how many hours he had devoted to writing and how he had become enraged when the computer didn't respond to his prompts. The memoir both obsessed and thrilled him.

Now that his memoir was mine, I hesitated to open it. I did not want to abuse the power I had from having outlived him. He would not have forgiven me. I wanted to let it sit for a while by itself, to allow it to feel at home in my house. Edgar was still too present. I felt it was still stamped with his bar code. Then, one long Saturday afternoon, I picked it up and rushed through it to the end, stopping only to make pencil marks in the margins. I did not want to pause too long for fear of getting caught, or rather, I told myself, for interrupting the flow. Then it sat untouched for three months as I moved it from table to chair to coffee table to end table and sometimes covered it with a pile of newspapers.

"We must do something with it," Sarah, his partner, and I finally agreed. "At least for the family."

We concurred that selling it to a publisher would be difficult. "Thank You For My Green Card" is the title of his immigrant story, one that has already been told in different ways at different times. A Swiss citizen's story is not likely to resonate with the new generation of immigrants from Latin America and Asia. But, we agreed—the pages sang. I heard his voice, saw his colorful descriptions, shared his feelings. We began to edit.

Edgar wrote well, he was a Pulitzer Prize-winning journalist, but his memoir revealed what both Sarah and I already knew: that he was a private man. No memoir appears complete for those who are close to the writer. Just as we cannot see ourselves accurately in the mirror, we cannot portray ourselves as others see us.

Sometimes we were tough on Edgar and excised an entire paragraph. It was redundant; it didn't fit in. Other times we succumbed to his persuasiveness. I wasn't upset by what he wrote about me, but I was upset by what he left out. When he described the aftermath of the automobile accident that instantly killed his wife, Louise, and almost took his own life, he mentioned his loyal visitors: Sargent Shriver, his

Washington colleagues, his doctors and kind nurses, but not me. And not our mother, who kept a vigil by his bedside. Every week for the three months he was hospitalized, I had gotten a baby sitter for the day and taken the two-hour bus trip to Hanover to be with him. On the day of Louise's funeral, I was not sure I should attend; he might die while I was away. But I should not feel hurt. It's natural to take family for granted.

Editing Edgar's memoir, page by page, sentence by sentence, I wanted to get closer to him. I wanted to ask him again about my father. Edgar was four years older than me and had memories that I did not. When I asked him a year before he died what he could tell me about our father, his reply was the same as always: "I don't remember." He did remember, though; he had to. He was seven years old. But Edgar had sealed up those memories as if they might seep poisonous fumes. Was my father harsh, even abusive? Or was Edgar still angry with him because he felt abandoned by his suicide—a hurt that does not recede over time? It must have been too painful to expose the wound, but in protecting himself, he deprived me of memories. Or was he protecting me from seeing a portrait of my father that was ugly? I push that thought away.

How is it possible, at the age of eighty-one, to still mourn my father, to seek my brother's memories? Two years after Edgar's death, he is entering my thoughts even more often than he did during the first year. I miss him as a presence a phone call away, as an ever-faithful participant on the Jewish holidays, as a raconteur, as a confidant, as a significant, glamorous, and caring uncle to my children. I sense his presence and his absence deeply. I want him to know what I know. I still have the urge to share things with him, like the celebration of John's ninetieth birthday, the election of Donald Trump, the defeat of Hillary Clinton. I turn around to tell him, and he's not there. Mourning does not have an end point. I have not stopped grieving for the father I did not know, or for the brother I did know.

I know I should be satisfied with what Edgar gave me. I can still feel him covering my hand with his and squeezing it as we sit in the synagogue on our last Yom Kippur together. I can hear his voice as I move his words around. He is there, both when I wish he would go away and let Sarah and me do our work and when I want him there, right between us, telling us to do less talking and more editing, to get the book done so that his story will be told.

As Edgar got older, he lost many things: his glasses, his phone. He couldn't find his address book so many times that when he called me, it often was because he had lost an address or a phone number and needed my help. But he always kept the same wallet. How do men manage to keep their wallets so thin, thin enough to slip into a back pocket or a vest pocket as easily as a cotton handkerchief?

When Edgar was moved to hospice in Tucson, the hospital nurse handed me his wallet. She had been keeping it in a locked cabinet while he was semiconscious in bed, oblivious to the need for identification. What do I do with it now that he's dead? If I open it I feel like a thief. It is still his. I stealthily count the bills. There are no large ones. A mugger would be disappointed. There is just enough for some groceries and perhaps a bottle of wine.

I sniff the leather. It smells as if he has just breathed on it. It is satin smooth, rubbed and oiled by the play of his fingers. I open it and find one credit card. That was enough for him. He did not like to spend money. I can barely read the gray numbers on his social security card, and I wonder if he received it with his first job. Another card is from the Pima County Public Library, a recent red and yellow identity I had not known about. There are no photos. He didn't carry the people he loved on his person. He must not have felt the need.

Or possibly he did not want to be reminded of his lost loves: his first wife, or his second.

Edgar enters my mind and sits there, like he would sit on the patch of lawn overlooking the lake. He would let the newspaper find its own gravity, lean his head back, and let sun seep into each pore as if it were life-giving. His recklessness made me worry about skin cancer, but he ignored me. The delicious warmth was worth any risk.

He was right. Cancer was not the culprit. Neither was diabetes, which he had suffered from for some forty years. I would scold him—without effect—when he insisted on taking a second piece of pie or piled on another spoonful of whipped cream. He would smack his lips and smile and say, "I'll just take more insulin."

It's hard to know precisely what caused his death. I think he decided to leave. The party was over. He was pleased with his life. The doctor diagnosed a mild case of pneumonia at the end. A CAT scan revealed a series of small strokes that enabled him to sleep much of the time in his last days. He welcomed the end and told us so. "This is a sanctified death," he breathed. I nodded and kissed his forehead.

𝒞 PLANETS

Seven new planets
circling a star
named Trappist-1,
forty light-years
from our earth.
Swirling globules
all in a row,
there may be water;
there may be life.
I am entranced,
curious like
a wide-eyed child:
another earth,
another life,
I will not know.
I will not live
long enough.
I will not know
my newborn granddaughter
when she falls in love.

14

My Fleeting Senses

❦

I CONFESS I FEEL A SENSE OF SATISFACTION
when I stand up quickly from the table without
holding on to the arms of my chair, as I watch
other Wake Robin residents do. The chairs have small,
clever wheels that make the turn away from the table
easier, even for me. I question whether I am guilty
of arrogance when I stride out of the dining room
without a cane, a walker, or a wheelchair, unlike my
gravity-bound husband, whose walker (and now, a
wheelchair) asks me to slowly navigate around chairs
and tables and out the door.

John hates his wheelchair. He hates being confined to a seated position while everyone else is standing. He hates not being able to make eye contact, not being able to join the conversation without great effort, and he hates being dependent on me—dependent on everyone. He can't move without me. Sometimes his trapped anger bursts out: "Damn, damn, damn!" So I time my pace to his. I am held back by an invisible sash at my waist. When I untie it, I flout my freedom like a puppy unleashed.

I can empathize with John. The signs are undeniable. Age is eroding my senses. Even when I wear my hearing aids, I don't catch every word in a movie theatre or a crowded room. Neither can I always answer a question from the audience without asking the person to repeat themselves. The sound seems loud enough, but I miss clarity.

I say "pardon me" more often than I used to. I console myself by thinking of the "Aging Tsunami" up ahead—and how they (whoever they may be) will soon create a more powerful hearing aid that catches every whisper. But it's likely hearing loss runs in my family. My brother had it and would often lose his hearing aids. He would recall visiting my grandmother as a small boy and being forced to stand at her bedside and shout into her enormous hearing horn.

Occasionally I am tempted to tune out an entire conversation and retreat into my own little sound-sealed world. Hearing loss can lead to mistakes when guessing what the sound means; coming out with one false word can be either hysterical or cruelly embarrassing, but I am aware of the danger of that kind of self-imposed loneliness.

I have learned to say, "Can you repeat that, please?" and to avoid, as much as possible, noisy places. A quiet restaurant, at my age, is a good restaurant. No matter how many stars a restaurant has earned, what matters to me, in my eighties, is the noise level. I have a fantasy about opening a Quiet Restaurant. In my restaurant, there would be no music and the interior would be plush: heavy drapes, thick carpets, and a padded ceiling to smother the sound. My customers would be able to hear one another without having to shout or repeat themselves again and again. This dream restaurant would develop a reputation as a place where people share secrets without fear of being overheard at the next table. Gossip about the neighbors' pending divorce, touch and go business deals, political forecasts, even personal confessions could be spilled out on the table. My Quiet Restaurant would show its age preference: more people over sixty-five would peruse the menus through their reading glasses than under. But I

won't worry, because in a few years those younger people will be lined up at the door, adjusting their own
hearing aids.

Sometimes I can't hear well because my hearing
aides have been forgotten at home. My friends who are
my age have endless stories to tell about losing things.
We try to console one other: "Oh, that happens to
me all the time." Neither can I find my passport-size
calendar that I keep in my purse, or my reading glasses.
I sometimes miss an appointment because I can't
decipher my own handwriting. I know I should keep
that information on my phone, but it's too complicated
and takes too much time.

I know that short-term memory loss is creeping up
on me like a hungry vine. Last spring I had a new experience. I bought a pound of asparagus at the Farmer's
Market on a Saturday morning. By Sunday afternoon,
I had lost my asparagus. I looked in all the obvious
places: kitchen counters, every cupboard, the refrigerator—even on top of the refrigerator. I calmed myself.
No one would steal a paper bag loaded with one pound
of asparagus.

Three days later, I found my missing vegetables.
They were still in the brown paper bag, the stalks
now slightly shriveled, in my husband's study beside
his computer. They had been waiting patiently to be

cooked. I questioned whether dementia was creeping up on me. I reassured myself again that losing a
bunch of asparagus must be a once in a lifetime event.
It wouldn't happen again. But I search for my phone
at least three times a day, sometimes more, sometimes
less. I deliberately bought a bright red case so I'd see it
when I left it on the couch, the coffee table, or in the
dark depths of my handbag. And if I still can't find it, I
know enough to call myself so the phone will call me,
and we'll be reunited.

I always (almost always) keep my phone in the side
pocket of my handbag. This location has many virtues:
I can touch it when I'm driving. It's easy to pull out of
its hiding place, and it's equally easy to return to its den.
But, I confess, sometimes it's the last place I remember
to look. Sometimes my phone is coy and plays hide-
and-seek under a newspaper, or even between its pages.
Or it will sit quietly behind a pillow or slide into my
coat pocket feigning sleep. If I were to add up the minutes I spend every day searching for it, I could finish a
short novel.

🎵 New Year's Eve at Wake Robin

The wheelchair danced in circles
to the rapid beat of the
Onion River Jazz Band.
She was young again,
unbound, free,
no longer pushing him,
but flying with him
on the dance floor.
He waved aside the
ribboned oxygen tube
streaming behind him.
I grasped John with both hands
And brought him to his feet,
placing the walker within reach.
He moved his head, and then his arms,
and then his feet to the music.
We danced, we sang,
with the walker between us,
and love inside us.

15

How Will I Die?

℮

L IVING AT WAKE ROBIN, I have become familiar with different ways of dying. A long-stemmed red rose announces a death. It is placed on a small table with a photograph in the foyer where it can't be missed. Residents stop and look and ask, "Who died?"

Dick Walters chose his own way to die. John and I visited him twenty-six hours before he was to take the drink that would kill him. He was watching television with the sound off. His wife, Ginny, sat beside him. They held hands like two teenagers. Was she, like him, ready to let go? They had done everything together, including lobbying for ten years for the passage of the Patient Choice and Control at the End of Life Act. They stood together next to the governor when he signed the act into law.

"Congratulations, Dick!" the crowd shouted in a chorus.

And now it was Dick's time to die by the hand that he had scripted. Two o'clock the next day, he would be in his room, surrounded by his family. He did not look as if he was at death's threshold. He was, by any measure, a happy man. He was ninety but could pass for seventy-five except for the oxygen tube plugged into his nose and curled down into his lap. Lung cancer was the culprit.

I observed Dick in his final hours. He behaved like a busy person in his office, answering his phone and responding to emails. I detected euphoria in his glittery eyes. He had determined that his time had come. It was a rude defeat for the devil. Dick would have the last word.

We had entered the apartment quietly. Dick gestured to us. "Come and sit down over here."

Everybody brought a dish. It was Ginny who added, "Can I get you something to drink?"

Nuts were offered. It felt wrong to take a handful and chew in his presence. Dick and Ginny told us about the wonderful family dinner they had eaten the night before. He was thrilled that his two granddaughters had come. They said it was like a birthday party.

The phone rang as we were leaving and I could hear Dick laugh, a deep chest laugh that I could recognize anywhere. Would I ever have the courage to follow his example if I had a terminal illness? I don't know.

My best friend, Nicky, had a different death. She died slowly at Wake Robin, so slowly that when I visited her in her last few months, I wished that she would have died sooner. It was difficult to understand her speech. There were moments of clarity when she knew who I was but then she would disappear into her cavern. She received kind physical care at Wake Robin but she was distraught—a butterfly caught in a net for months.

When Nicky was wheeled into the dining room I sat across from her. She wore a bib. I could not tell if she was hungry or not, but when I brought the spoon to her lips, she opened her red mouth like a little bird without a chirp. Despite knowing that food would prolong her life, my mouth opened when hers did. I believed food was good for her.

"Dear God," I said to myself. "Let me die before this happens to me."

Louise died as she wished. She was suffering from the ravages of a stroke. She stopped eating. Then she changed her mind and announced that she wanted to live a bit longer to find out what would happen to Senator Bernie Sanders in the Democratic primary against Hillary Clinton. Louise had always been a progressive liberal, but with an overlay of class. She had lost a son in Vietnam, and that was how we met, at the Vietnam Memorial on Interstate 89. She had demonstrated against the war passionately. Then, when her husband was transferred with IBM to Vermont, she became a passionate advocate for prison reform. The Sanders campaign dragged out longer than Louise's desire to live. She could no longer find any joy in life.

"Louise is dying," my friend Betty told me.

The straight, narrow fold in the bed was Louise. I bent down and spoke to her. "I'm here. This is Madeleine. You're leaving. It's okay. We love you," and I let go of her hand.

She mouthed words back to me with surprising force. She wanted to talk. She may have made a last pitch for Bernie, for all I know. Contrary to what many might think, starvation at the end of life is not painful. She died three days later, in peace. Still, it is not easy.

How will I die? Will I be like Dick, Nicky, or Louise? Or will I be lucky enough to die like Marilyn, who turned around to go home as she was walking downtown with her husband. She had indigestion. She was sitting on the couch when she took her last breath. Gone. Ideal.

Lately, colon cancer has been ranking first in my list of anxieties, because I have irritable bowel syndrome. My large intestine has a mind of its own. It is often cross, and I suffer from abdominal cramps. I never paid attention to my colon until I got older; it functioned fine without me. Then, after a colonoscopy ten years ago, I was informed that I had a "redundant colon," which means that it loops around twice and has to work twice as hard. That may be why it sputters and groans so much. On bad days, my worst fear is that a tumor may be snuggling inside the double coils and growing quietly. I think of my cousin, who almost died from an intestinal blockage and arrived at the hospital just in time for surgery. Or, I wonder, are my intestinal problems caused by stress? I know there is a brain-gut connection, but how do I control it? Lack of certainty opens the maw of worry wide.

I worry less now about lung cancer, even though I used to be a smoker. It's been forty-two years since I quit. I started smoking when female film stars untangled their complicated love lives with cigarettes in their beautiful hands. Stars even appeared in cigarette advertisements. Their smoky, sexy portraits pulled me in. I wanted to be like them. I had my first cigarette when I was sixteen or seventeen, along with my first mixed drink: a daiquiri. I felt extremely sophisticated as I posed on a barstool facing my date, Kenny.

Smoking was a way to announce my independence and step over the threshold of youth into adulthood. Then I turned to throat-scratching Gauloises Bleues and pretended to be French when I was a guide at the Brussels World's Fair in 1958. Soon smoking became a habit. I could not write, or even think, without a cigarette. I seem to have escaped the ultimate punishment for that indulgence—so far. But when I get out of breath walking up a familiar hill, one that never taxed me before I turned eighty, I wonder if the ashes of those long-ago cigarettes still rest inside me.

Flying is not a new fear for me. I never liked to fly, but because I have flown so much in my career, I am getting better at it. I know that it is unlikely my life will end by falling out of the sky. Still, my palms sweat when there is turbulence. My body fights back against the plane's rattles and shakes. I try to inhale and exhale slowly and lecture to myself that the pilot wants to stay alive as much as I do. But what if he doesn't? In 2015, when a Lufthansa airliner plunged headfirst into the French Alps, it was flown by a suicidal pilot.

I understand (sort of) how cars move, but I don't know how airplanes fly. The sky is wide open, a mysterious ether with no perceptible speed limits, no white lines. I know that pilots are told by air controllers to fly at certain heights, and even stay within certain lanes. The trouble is, I can't see them. If there were chalk marks in the sky, I could easily peel my fingers off the armrest and "enjoy my flight." Lately, whenever the captain announces that the flight attendants should stop serving drinks, sit down, and buckle up because of expected turbulence, I tell myself that I am ready to die. I have lived a good life. In my mind, I begin to write my obituary. I wonder, will my death make the headlines? Then the air becomes smooth again, and I take it all back.

Driving a car is no doubt the most dangerous thing anyone can do, and I am more conscious of the risks now that I am over eighty. What if I put my foot down on the gas pedal instead of the brake; what if I don't turn my head around far enough (because it hurts) when backing up? My worst fear is not my own death but killing someone else: a bicyclist pedaling up the road or a child running across the street. I sometimes rush through a yellow light and then chastise myself midway across the intersection as it turns red. I am no longer young. Drive carefully, drive slowly, I remind myself, even as I suspect that the person in the car behind me complains that I'm driving "like an old lady."

I no longer like to drive at night. One evening, going north on two-lane Route 7 at twilight, the sky turned from blue to black too soon. It became harder to follow the tire-scuffed white lines where the asphalt shoulder turns into dirt. I shifted my eyes slightly to the right of center to avoid the direct glare of oncoming cars. It seemed as if every car had its brights on and aiming directly for my startled pupils. My eyes adjusted slowly, too slowly, I feared. I was afraid to look up at the stars. As night's blanket folded over the road, I saw small squares of yellow light glued onto black houses. I thought of the families inside, clearing the dishes, or already sitting in the living room watching TV. There might be a fire, a curled-up cat, a sleeping dog. Soon they would go upstairs to a nice warm bed. I envied them. They were home.

A stroke could happen anytime, anywhere—a marble-sized blood clot traveling through my body and then, pow, it hits my brain. I try to recall the diagrams of the heart that I memorized in high school and have not thought about since. I have no idea how strong my aorta is, or the condition of my jugular vein. I take a steady flow of blood to my heart for granted until I encounter a friend being pushed down the hall in a wheelchair at Wake Robin. I say hello. She smiles a crooked smile back.

Some strokes are baby strokes and leave little evidence of their impact. Others are like a tornado ripping through the body, leaving destruction and silence in their wake. Please God, spare me. Don't leave me half alive, or half dead, I pray. An easy death, a good death, is what I wish for, just like everyone else.

Old Age. The two words together shock me. Am I there yet? But I am not really old, not as old as she is, who needs help dressing, not as old as he is, rolling slowly past me in his wheelchair. I live independently. I don't need a walker. I can walk upstairs and down (okay, my knees hurt a little). I can hear (with the help of new hearing aids) and see (just reading glasses). I take pills, yes, but not that many.

I know that death is close, but life is always closer. Although my future no longer feels infinite, it is filled with possibilities that I want to explore. As long as I'm curious about what will happen next, how things work, how the world works, I want to be alive. I try to cultivate awareness, what Buddhists call "mindfulness." But of course, it's impossible to practice it all day long. My mind wanders after three minutes, drawn to the blooming sunset spreading across the horizon while I cover my husband's hand with mine. I focus for one minute when my tongue tastes a delicious salad, or another minute or two when I sidestroke in the cold waters of Lake Champlain and feel reborn. Savoring moments. Giving thanks, to someone, or something, even God. Perhaps that's enough. Maybe I'll get better at this with time. It may be one of the unanticipated benefits of old age: experiencing an intense love for life with only a tinge of regret. I don't believe in life after death, although it is tempting to believe that I will meet my parents and grandparents, Edgar, and all my loved ones in heaven. It would be a crowded reunion. When I am close to death, I hope I will have someone hold my hand. Then I will let go, say farewell to life, and go to sleep in peace, as if I were resting on a cloud.

ℰ Last Spring

First the daffodils die,
then the tulips stiffen,
then the lilacs' perfume
turns bitter brown,
and the peonies slump
to their graves.
I mourn them,
each one,
like I never did before.

16

The Lake

ॐ

THE LAKE FEELS LIKE A BODY, subject to reconfiguration by any change in light, wind, and temperature. Some nights when I can't fall asleep, I calm my mind by visualizing its smooth sea and synchronizing my breath with its rhythm. Other nights the lake is capable of giving me nightmares. More than once I saw a black and white sea pound at the foundation of our house or smash against our sliding glass doors. Bits of wooden siding fall into the ravenous sea. Other nights I am a figure in a Japanese print watching a white-frilled tsunami swim toward our beach. Waves threaten to eat their way into the house. I wake up with my heart pounding, followed by relief. It has only been a dream.

Each day, often each hour, the lake changes its contours to obey the wind, the master choreographer who orders it to lie flat as a floor or to rise like soup bubbling over. And so, I watch the lake's body change, slimming down twenty, thirty, or sixty feet from the shore in the fall and gaining all its pounds back in the spring like a woman on a failed diet.

As I prepare my departure from the lake, I tell myself that I should have devoted more hours to looking at it, doing nothing but looking. I'm a remorseful lover. I wish I had said "I love you" more often. I seldom took the time to sit and stare, except on those few hot days when I would allow myself a half an hour to sit at the beach and gaze. I console myself with the understanding that I will have visitation rights at public beaches, though the lake will no longer be mine.

Submerging myself the first thing in the morning feels like a baptism. The lake pulls me in, filled with eons of accumulation of minerals and flotsam and jetsam. It has been laid down layer upon layer and it will continue to build long after human life disappears.

In the lake I measure progress against the shore. But the lake is deceptive. When I swim against the waves,

I cannot tell if I am moving or if I am swimming in place. I am a humbling dot. The lake has boundaries, but they are so expansive that I remain a small creature.

The lake is indifferent. It does not care if I keep on swimming or sink to my death. "Those are pearls that were his eyes," wrote Shakespeare. But I am not ready for a watery death.

ꙮ A Love Poem

Each night
I wheel you to your door
with a kiss on your lips.
I smile my love at you,
generously, I think.
You don't know how much I love
you, you say.
I do, I do.
We've formed a ritual
of waving goodbye as I retreat
slowly down the hall.
At first, I wave with one
hand in the air, and then
my arms go wild before
I turn the corner,
as if struck by a storm
or signaling for help.
We wave in tandem.
You are there, and I
am here.

The nurses now know
we wave not for them,
but for one another;
to have and to hold
the love we swore to
once and forever.

ꝗ

ON JANUARY 21, 2017, I spoke at the Women's
March in Montpelier on the steps in front of
the Vermont State House. There were ten to
twenty thousand people assembled below. The State
Police had to close the interstate exit to prevent more
people from coming because traffic had clogged the
streets.

One day after President Trump was sworn into
office, women marched who never had marched before.
They became instant activists because of Trump's
frightening campaign promises, including the repeal of
Roe vs. Wade and the destruction of the Affordable
Care Act. Vermont held one of 633 women's marches

that took place around the world. The march in Washington was the largest protest in a single day in history.

Some observers questioned the march's impact—that it would be destined to be a one-time event, that women would pack up their signs and go home.

They were wrong.

ॐ

THE SURGE OF ACTIVISM that burst out of the marches has not died. One indicator is the record number of women who are running for office. And several have upset long-time incumbents. Change is happening where it never surfaced before. For example, the teachers' strikes last spring in several conservative states resulted in teachers winning higher wages and increased funding for school supplies. And the MeToo movement has toppled sexual abusers off their pedestals at a dizzying rate.

But the rate of devastating decisions made by the president—from his Supreme Court nomination to his separation of immigrant children from their parents—has left many women and men outraged, but fatigued. I am often asked: "Tell me, what can we do?"

I give a short-term and a long-term answer. One, continue to protest, because sometimes it works. The

Trump family separation policy was stopped (but not fixed) after members of both parties expressed outrage. The answer is that we must continue to take to the streets the old-fashioned way. Be vocal and visible. The long-term answer is at the ballot box. Organize, vote, register voters, and get out the vote. It sounds simple, but it's hard work.

THE FOLLOWING IS THE SPEECH I gave at the march in Montpelier. The spirit of the Women's March cannot flag. Women are beginning to turn their outrage against injustice into action in the workplace, the home, and the community. We cannot stop now.

Hello Everybody, Sisters, and Brothers,

What a beautiful sight you are. It's like spring has arrived in Vermont and thousands of flowers are blooming in front of the State House. I feel a "crowd hug."

We are not alone in our fear; we are not alone in our despair; we are not alone in our grief for what might have been. We are together in our strength, together in our power, and together we march. Why do we march? We march for *respect*.

We march for equal pay.
We march for the right to control our bodies.
We march for a livable planet.
We march for the end of violence against women.
We march for health care for all.
We march for public education.
We march for the Constitution and the Bill of Rights.

And who are we? We are brown, black, yellow, and white. We are gay, straight, transgender, and queer. We are wives, mothers, grandmothers, singles, sisters, daughters, and lovers. We are teachers, students, professors, waitresses, sales clerks, bartenders, nurses, doctors, artists, lawyers, farmers, factory workers, cooks, and caregivers. And we are immigrants.

We are here to pledge to be our sister's and brother's keepers. And we are here because women's rights are human rights, and human rights are women's rights, all over the world. Can we do this? Will we make a difference? Have we got the power?

The pendulum has swung so fast from Obama to Trump that we are experiencing whiplash. I assure it will swing back again—when we push hard. We have a rock to stand on. It is called Democracy. It is called the Constitution. The center will hold.

But, only if we are vigilant. Only if we use our voices and our feet. We must demonstrate that there is another America. An America that looks like us, that thinks like us, that believes in the America that we believe in.

It is we who make America.
It is we who make America great.
We are the makers, the doers, the dreamers.
We are the citizens who have the power of the vote.

In the next four years, we will be heard, not only in this place, at this time, but throughout the land, in towns and cities and in our nation's capital, and all over the world where people are marching with us.

We pledge not to be silent.
We pledge not to be interrupted.
We pledge not to be sidelined.
We pledge not to be stopped.
We pledge not to be afraid,
and we pledge not to *lose hope*.

We must keep hope alive. I will read the first stanza of a poem called "Hope" by Emily Dickinson.

> *Hope is a thing with feathers*
> *That perches in the soul*
> *And sings the tune without the words*
> *And never stops at all.*

About the Author

Twenty-five years ago, Madeleine Kunin became the first woman to be elected governor of Vermont, serving three terms. She was American ambassador to Switzerland and U.S. deputy secretary of education. Madeleine Kunin has written three previous books: *Living a Political Life* (Knopf), *The New Feminist Agenda: Defining the Next Revolution for Women, Work, and Family* (*New York Times* Editor's Choice), and *Pearls Politics and Power*. She has more energy than two forty year olds. She is currently James Marsh Professor-at-Large at the University of Vermont, where she gives guest lectures on feminism, women, and politics. She also serves on the board of the Institute for Sustainable Communities (ISC), a nongovernmental organization that she founded in 1991, and she recently launched Emerge Vermont to encourage and support women in politics. She lives in Shelburne, Vermont.

Coming of Age was typeset in Minion. In designing Minion font, Robert Slimbach was inspired by the timeless beauty of the fonts of the late Renaissance. Minion was created primarily as a traditional text font but adapts well to today's digital technology, presenting the richness of the late baroque forms within modern text formats. This clear, balanced font is suitable for almost any use. The name comes from the traditional naming system for type sizes, in which minion is between nonpareil and brevier, with the type body 7pt in height. As the name suggests, it is particularly intended as a font for body text in a classical style, neutral and practical while also slightly condensed to save space. Slimbach described the design as having "a simplified structure and moderate proportions." The ornaments, or dingbats, used throughout the text are also from the Minion family.

∾

DESIGN BY DEDE CUMMINGS
BRATTLEBORO, VERMONT